# FOUR POINT
## Listening and Speaking

# 1

Darren Tong

# FOUR POINT
## Listening and Speaking

### 1
#### INTERMEDIATE

## KEITH S. FOLSE
University of Central Florida

## ROBYN BRINKS LOCKWOOD
Stanford University

Series Editor: KEITH S. FOLSE

Ann Arbor
University of Michigan Press

Copyright © by the University of Michigan 2010
All rights reserved
Published in the United States of America
The University of Michigan Press
Manufactured in the United States of America

∞ Printed on acid-free paper

ISBN-13: 978-0-472-03355-3

2013    2012    2011    2010                4        3        2        1

# Acknowledgments

Robyn is grateful to:

Keith Folse, co-author and series editor, for his valuable feedback and input.

Kelly Sippell, one of the best editors in the business, for her support and hard work.

Dr. Virgil Brinks and Mrs. June Brinks, her parents, two amazing teachers who taught her how to develop ideas for the classroom.

Countless students along the way for trying ideas.

Keith would like to thank Kelly Sippell, our editor at the University of Michigan Press, his TESOL students, and the teachers who make this profession what it is.

The publisher, series editor, and authors would like to thank the educational professionals whose reviews helped shape the Four Point series, particularly those from these institutions:

Auburn University
Boston University CELOP
Central Piedmont Community College
Colorado State University
Daytona Beach Community College
Duke University
Durham Technical College
Georgia State University
Harding University
Hillsborough Community College
Northern Virginia Community College, Alexandria Campus
Oregon State University
University of California, San Diego
University of Nevada at Las Vegas
University of North Carolina, Charlotte
Valencia Community College

The University of Michigan Press thanks:

Bridget Bodnar, Pat Grimes, Joseph Jasina, Morgan Peterson, and Karen Pitton for their voices (audio); Jake Christensen, Dana Dembowski, Scott Ham, Joseph Jasina, Morgan Peterson, and Tong Serena Wu for their acting (video).

Elie Mosseri of Mosseri Enterprises, Fred Goryzk (video), and Doug Trevethan (video and audio) for production of the audio and video that accompany this book.

*Grateful acknowledgment is made to the following authors, publishers, and individuals for permission to reprint copyrighted or previously published materials.*

Jupiter Unlimited for photos.

Library of Congress for photo of suffragettes.

*Every effort has been made to contact the copyright holders for permission to reprint borrowed material. We regret any oversights that may have occurred and will rectify them in future printings of this book.*

# Contents

# Series Overview

*Four Point* is a four-volume series designed for English language learners whose primary goal is to succeed in an academic setting. While grammar points and learning strategies are certainly important, academic English Language Learners (ELLs) need skills-based books that focus on the four primary skills of reading, writing, listening, and speaking in a realistic, integrated format, as well as the two primary language bases of vocabulary and grammar. To this end, the *Four Point* series offers a unique combination of instructional material and activities that truly require students to read, write, speak, and listen in a multitude of combinations.

*Four Point* has two levels. Level 1 is upper-intermediate (TOEFL® PBT 440–480). Book 2 is advanced (TOEFL® PBT 480–520). While academic listening and speaking skills are covered in one volume and academic reading and writing are covered in another, *all four skills are integrated throughout all books,* so a given task may focus on speaking and listening but have a reading and/or writing component to it as well.

## Developing the Four Skills in *Four Point*

The series covers the four academic skills of reading, writing, listening, and speaking,  while providing reinforcement and systematic recycling of key vocabulary issues and further exposure to grammar issues. The goal of this series is to help students improve their ability in each of these four critical skills and thereby enable the students to have sufficient English to succeed in their final academic setting, whether it be high school, community college, college, or university.

Many ELLs report great difficulties upon entering their academic courses after they leave the safe haven of their English class with other nonnative speakers and their sympathetic and caring ESL teachers. Their academic instructors speak quickly, give long reading assignments due the next day, deliver classroom lectures and interactions at rapid, native speed, and sometimes balk at the excessive errors in their ELLs' writing. In sum, the ELL who has gone through a sheltered classroom setting is in for a rather rude awakening in a new learning situation where English is taken for granted and no one seems to understand or care much about the new reality of dilemmas of ELLs. Through these materials, we hope to lessen the shock of such an awakening.

The activities in *Four Point* achieve the goal of helping ELLs experience what life beyond the ESL classroom is like while they are still in a sheltered classroom. This chart explains some of the activities in *Four Point*:

| Reading | Listening |
|---|---|
| Students will read longer, more difficult readings on interesting academic topics that represent the array of interests in a classroom. Extensive pleasure reading is good, but ELLs need practice for the type of reading they will find in their academic course books as well. | Students will have to listen to both short and long lectures to not only pick out details and facts but also practice picking up on speaker intentions or attitudes. Students will also gain experience listening to multiple native speakers at the same time. |
| **Writing** | **Speaking** |
| Students will write both short and long assignments that can be organized around more traditional writing templates such as the model paragraph or five-paragraph essay. | Students will practice both short and long extemporaneous speaking and thereby develop their speaking fluency, an area often overlooked in many ESL books. Students will also practice interrupting, maintaining the floor, and adding speech to another speaker's ideas on the spot. |

## Maximizing Coverage of the Two Primary Language Bases

ESL materials have come a long way from the old days of equating repetitive grammar drills for speaking practice or copying sentences for writing practice. However, in the ensuing shift from focus on language to focus on communication, very little was developed to address the needs of academic ELLs who need to do much more in English than engage in conversations about daily events, fill out job applications, or read short pieces of text for pleasure. It was the proverbial "baby being thrown out with the bath water" as emphasis on grammar and vocabulary was downplayed. However, in order to participate in academic settings, our ELLs certainly need focused activities to develop and then maintain their use of vocabulary and grammar. Toward this end, the *Four Point* series provides further exposure of key grammar issues without overt practice activities.

More important, these books focus very heavily on vocabulary because ELLs realize that they are way behind their native-speaker counterparts when it comes to vocabulary. Each book highlights between 125–150 key vocabulary items, including individual words, compound words, phrasal verbs, short phrases, idioms, metaphors, collocations, and longer set lexical phrases. In learning vocabulary, the two most important features are frequency of retrievals (i.e., in exercises) and the spacing between these retrievals. Spaced rehearsal is accomplished in two ways. First, after words appear in a textbook, they will reappear multiple times afterward. Second, interactive web-based exercises provide more than ample opportunities for ELLs to practice their vocabulary learning through spaced rehearsals at the student's convenience (www.press.umich.edu/esl/compsite/4Point/).

## General Overview of Units

Each of the books is divided into six units with numerous activities within each unit. The material in each of the volumes could be covered in ten to twelve weeks, but this number is flexible depending on the students and the teacher, and the depth to which the material is practiced.

## Using the Exercises in This Book

Each unit includes two lectures on the same topic within a field of academic study. The exercises accompanying the lectures are meant to strengthen a range of listening and speaking skills, notably:

- understanding main ideas
- comprehending details
- understanding classroom discourse
- using academic language functions
- recognizing signal words and phrases
- developing vocabulary
- synthesizing information

In addition to more general listening comprehension tasks, most units include a specific listening focus, such as listening for persuasion, listening for definition cues, or listening for numbers. The lectures range in length from approximately four to seven minutes. In addition, most of the other tasks are between three and five minutes, offering practice with longer, connected discourse that students need to build listening comprehension skills. Lectures and other material are provided on the audio CD packaged with the book. Six video clips can be found online at www.press.umich.edu/esl/compsite/4Point/

## Pre-Listening Activities

A range of pre-listening discussion questions is included; each has the purpose of activating prior knowledge about and generating interest in the topics in the unit. Often these questions provide opportunities for students to anticipate content and, therefore, may be revisited throughout the unit. All of the pre-listening tasks lead to pair or small group discussions.

## Note-Taking Strategies

Each unit introduces a note-taking strategy, allowing students to develop a repertoire of techniques to choose from in their studies. As students preferences vary, it is important to supply them with options. It is certainly possible that students can draw on formats that work particularly well for them in one unit as they practice and develop their note-taking skills in another.

Other types of strategies and skills—those related to listening, speaking, and vocabulary—are highlighted at various points throughout the units. Each appears in a display box with a short explanation.

## Listening Activities

Each note-taking activity in a unit is followed by main idea and detailed comprehension questions. The main idea questions serve to help students summarize ideas from their notes. Students can listen to the lecture again as they complete the multiple choice questions for Check Your Understanding: Details. The listening passage allows students to practice the strategy and/or hear the signal words or phrases in use.

## Vocabulary Activities

Vocabulary Power activities appear once in each unit. The words chosen for these tasks are ones that may appear in a variety of academic settings. These activities serve to further check students' comprehension of the lecture. These words are likely to be useful to the students as they move on to the extensive speaking activities at the end of each unit: the Rapid Vocabulary Review, which focuses on synonyms and combinations and associations, and the Vocabulary Log. Students could also be asked to listen to portions of the lecture again to discover if they recognize the words used in context.

### In-Class Interactions/Classroom Discourse

In addition to the lectures, each unit includes activities based on the in-class interactions students are likely to encounter in post-secondary classrooms. Throughout the units, students participate in group activities that allow them to use the speaking phrases taught in the unit. Other activities include You Be the Judge, debates, and in-depth discussions. The resolutions to the You Be the Judge activities, the actual court cases, appear at the back of the book.

Six video clips are provided on the companion website (www.press.umich.edu/esl/compsite/4Point/) to analyze for language, tone, and nonverbal cues as well as generate discussion on academic listening and speaking tasks. Throughout the interaction, the students use many of the phrases and employ the strategies taught in the unit—and, in some cases, not using the best communication strategies. ELLs will have the opportunity to hear the phrases used in a natural conversation, practice their listening skills, analyze verbal and nonverbal communication skills of the students, and think critically about and discuss the interaction with their classmates. Questions in the book require students to listen for certain phrases and identify what they mean; notice the tone of voice and think about how it changes the dynamics of a discussion; recognize the influence of nonverbal communication by increasing their awareness of facial expressions, gestures, and other cues; and compile all of these ideas into an analytical discussion about the interaction in the video.

### Reading Tasks

Each unit includes a reading generally used as the impetus for more extensive speaking activities and as a way to practice the strategies. As such, they do not include detailed comprehension questions. As the topics in the units are current, the instructor could easily supplement a unit with current online readings.

### Synthesizing: Projects and Presentations

The summative task for each unit includes four projects that relate to the topic and encourage practice of the listening and speaking concepts. Students prepare projects and presentations based on what they have learned via the lectures, readings, discussions, or Internet or library research. For group projects, students should be given adequate time to clarify group roles and to work on their projects.

### Rapid Vocabulary Review and Vocabulary Log

A vocabulary review task appears at the end of each unit and gives students another opportunity to check their understanding of key words. The correct answer is a synonym or brief definition. Crucial to the vocabulary acquisition process is the initial noticing of unknown vocabulary. ELLs must notice the vocabulary in some way, and this noticing then triggers awareness of the item and draws the learner's attention to the word in all subsequent encounters, whether the word is read in a passage or heard in a conversation or lecture. To facilitate noticing and then multiple retrievals of new vocabulary, we have included a chart listing 25 key vocabulary items at the end of each unit. This Vocabulary Log has three columns and requires students to provide a definition or translation in the second column and then an original example or note about usage in the third column.

As demonstrated in *Vocabulary Myths* (Folse 2004, University of Michigan Press), there is no research showing that a definition is better than a translation or vice-versa, so we suggest that you let ELLs decide which one they prefer. After all, this log is each student's individual vocabulary notebook, so students should use whatever information is helpful to them and that will help them remember and use the vocabulary item. If the log information is not deemed useful, the learner will not review this material—which defeats the whole purpose of keeping the notebook. In the third column, students can use the word in a phrase or sentence, or they can also add usage information about the word such as *usually negative, very formal sounding,* or *used only with the word* launch, for example.

# Political Science:
## Elections

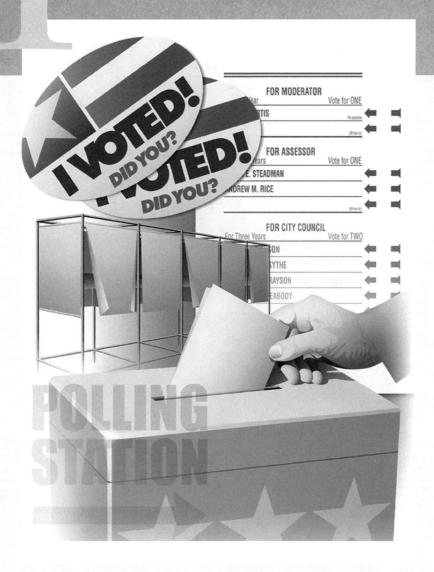

Political science is a social study concerned with government and its people, systems, and behaviors. One area of politics is elections, which is the act of choosing or selecting people to run the government. This unit explores different types of elections and common political issues.

# Part 1: Student Government

## Pre-Listening Activities

Many schools and universities have a student government comprised of student representatives and officers like a president, vice-president, and secretary, who are elected by the student body. The elected students are responsible for such things as representing the interests and concerns of the students, sponsoring programs and entertainment, and serving as a link between the administration and the students. Answer these questions with a partner.

1. What do you know about your school's student government? Do you know any officers? Did you vote in the election?

   _____

   _____

   _____

2. Would you want to run for the student government? Why or why not?

   _____

   _____

   _____

## Strategy: Listening for and Giving Numerical Information

In English, different patterns are used when giving numerical information.

### Location

If a room number or address is a single digit, say the one number.

> Room 6 [room six]
>
> 8 Wells Hall [eight Wells Hall]

If a room number or address has two digits, say the whole number (not two individual numbers)

> Room 62 [sixty-two] (not six two)
>
> 28 Wells Hall [twenty-eight] (not two eight)

If a room number or address has three digits, say the first as a single digit and pronounce the last two as a whole number. If the location has a number that is a multiple of one hundred, then pronounce it as such.

> Room 621 [six twenty-one]
>
> 234 Campus Drive [two thirty-four]
>
> 400 University Avenue [four hundred]

If a room number or address has four digits, say them as two whole numbers with a slight pause between them. If the location is a multiple of one thousand, then pronounce it as such.

> Room 6217 [sixty-two/pause/seventeen]
>
> 2845 Willow Drive [twenty-eight/pause/forty-five]
>
> 1000 Main Street [one thousand]

### Time

If a time is on the hour, we say the single digit.

> 7:00 [seven]

If the time is not on the hour, we say the hour as a single digit and the minutes as a whole number.

> 7:15 [seven fifteen]

If the number contains a zero, we usually pronounce it as "oh," not "zero."

> 7:04 [seven oh four]

## Phone Numbers

For the first part of the phone number (including the area code), say the first three digits as single or individual digits and then pause. For the last part of the phone number, say the first two as single digits, pause, and then say the last two as single digits.

> 555-2758 [five five five/pause/two seven/pause/five eight]

Another way to think about this is to say the numbers in terms of intonation as flat, flat, flat, (555); up, up, (27); down, down, (58).

Some people will pronounce the second part as two whole numbers with a pause between them.

> 555-2758 [five five five/pause/twenty-seven/pause/ fifty-eight]

If the second part has a teen number, say them as single digits or whole numbers, but do not combine single digits and whole numbers.

> 555-1628 [five five five/pause/sixteen/pause/twenty-eight] or [five five five/pause/one six/pause/two eight] (not five five five/pause/sixteen/pause/two eight)

If the number is a multiple of one thousand, say it as such.

> 555-1000 [five five five/pause/one thousand]

If the first part of the number contains a zero, it is common say it as "oh." If the second part of the number contains a zero, say it as "zero."

> 650-4008 [six five oh/pause/four zero zero eight]

*Pronunciation Note:* When pronouncing one of the teen numbers (13/thirteen through 19/nineteen), make sure the *t* sound is clear and your listener can hear the /n/ sound at the end of the word. When pronouncing a ten (or *-ty*) number that ends in zero (20/twenty to 90/ninety), the *t* will sound more like a *d*. Also notice that the syllable stress is different. The teens have the main stress on the second syllable. The tens are stressed on the first syllable. You can confirm the number by asking, "Did you say fifteen, one five, or fifty, five zero?"

## Listening for and Giving Numerical Information

Write any two room numbers, times, and phone numbers that you can think of or make up. Say them to a partner, expressing yourself clearly in English. Then exchange roles, and write your partner's numbers.

Your room numbers: _____ 2 65 _____ llc _____

Your times: _____ 17 : 10 _____

Your phone numbers: _____ 541 _____ 9797298 _____

Your partner's room numbers: 428 Northwest 19th street

Your partner's times: _____ 16 : 00 _____

Your phone numbers: _____ 541 9796238 _____

## Listening 1: Scheduling a Meeting for an Event

## Listening for Information

The listening passage is a conversation between two students. They are discussing the debate between candidates who are campaigning to be president of the student government. They use several numbers in the conversation when talking about time, location, and contact information. As you listen to the conversation, write answers to the questions.

1. What time does the debate start? _____ 7:00 _____

2. What time does the meet-the-candidates function start? _____ 6:30 _____

3. What time is the question period scheduled to begin? _____ 8:00 _____

4. Where is the meet-the-candidates function? Room 458 _____

5. Where is the debate? Room 460 _____ 321 lobby

6. Where is the reception? 52 lobby room 14

7. What time does the first student get off work? _____ 5:00 _____ 4:30

8. What is the second student's phone number? 555-8117

## Speaking

### Clarifying

Sometimes you want to make sure that you have heard something correctly or that you have understood the meaning. Using certain phrases to ask for clarification will help you make sure you have the correct information.

ASKING FOR CLARIFICATION

| About Specific Information | About General Information |
|---|---|
| *I didn't catch that* [street number and name]. | *I didn't catch what you said about. . .* |
| *Can you repeat that* [phone number]? | *I'm not sure I understand your last point.* |
| *I'm sorry, but I didn't get that* [room number]. *Would you say it again?* | *Are you saying that. . .* |
| *Did you say* [Room 621]? | *Do you mean that. . .* |
| *Could you spell that* [street number and name], *please?* | *So what exactly do you mean by that?* |
| *Could you say that slower, please?* | *Could you explain it again?* |

If you are the speaker and someone asks you for information, you will have to clarify or restate information. There are some common phrases to use to repeat or reword the information for the listener.

GIVING CLARIFICATION

| About Specific Information | About General Information |
|---|---|
| *That* [address] *was. . .* | *Let me say it another way.* |
| *Let me repeat that* [phone number]. *It was . . .* | *My point is that. . .* |
| *I'll say it again.* | *What I mean is. . .* |
| *No, I said* [Room 621]. | *In other words. . .* |
| *Yes, that's right.* | *I can make it clearer by saying. . .* |

## Role-Playing

Work with a classmate to role play possible conversations for this situation. Use the phrases in the boxes on page 6 or others that you can think of to write dialogues. Then read your dialogues for the class.

**SITUATION**

Kyle wants to be president of the student government. His competitor is leading in the polls because he is giving away free food at his rallies. During a campaign speech, Kyle promises the audience that he will work with university administrators to lower tuition by five percent. He knows this isn't possible, but he feels he will lose the election unless he makes this promise.

Person A begins by saying what will happen if the students find out that Kyle can't keep his promise.

Person B will ask for clarification about Person A's statement.

Person A will clarify and use other words.

Person A:

_____

Person B:

_____

Person A:

_____

Can you extend the conversation with other ideas and clarifications?

_____

_____

_____

_____

_____

## Asking for More Information

One of the best ways to get more information is to use *wh-* questions: *who, what, where, when,* and *why.* You can also ask questions beginning with the word *how.*

Student government representatives are responsible for being the voice of the students. Their platforms are an announcement of what principles will be the basis of their time in office. Candidates state what problems they will address and how they will solve them. Read the list of issues that may be part of a college or university presidential platform, and then write one question asking for more information about five of the issues.

| | |
|---|---|
| campus facilities | housing |
| campus safety | meal plan choices |
| communication with administrators | parking |
| communication with students | student activities |
| diversity | tuition |

Example:  housing issues
Question:  What do you plan to do about the crowded dormitories on campus? How do you plan to accomplish that?

Example:  campus facilities
Question:  When do you think the campus library should be open?

1. __What do you plan to do about (enhanced) campus safety?__
2. __When do you think campus safety is not safety enough__
3. __Where do you think need enhanced its safety__
4. __Who do you think responds.__
5. __why__

## Making an Impromptu Speech

Each student will be a presidential candidate for student body president. Look at the five questions you wrote and think about which is about the most important issue for you. You will have the chance to ask a classmate your question. Be prepared to answer one of their questions when it is your turn to run for president. You will have two minutes to answer the question and give specific details about your plan.

# Part 2: Discussing Serious Issues

## Pre-Listening Activities

As you learned in Part 1, college campuses often have a student government that addresses the needs and wants of the student body. On a larger scale, a city's or country's government looks at and makes decisions about citizens' needs and wants. Answer these questions with a partner.

1. What are common issues for a government you are familiar with?

   _economy_

   _____

   _____

2. Look at the list of issues that presidential candidates in the United States sometimes consider when developing their platform. Which do you consider the most important? Why?

   | | |
   |---|---|
   | civil rights | health care |
   | economy | international relations |
   | education | immigration |
   | environment | military |
   | gun control | taxes |

   _Civil rights,_

   _____

   _____

3. What other issues should the government address?

   _____

   _____

   _____

# Reading

One issue important to many people is service or volunteering. Read about some of the progress President Obama made and the general vision and principles he hoped for during his first year in office. Discuss his ideas as well as your own ideas about service and volunteering.

## Service

### *Progress*

On April 21, 2009, President Obama signed the Edward M. Kennedy Serve America Act, a hallmark piece of legislation.

- The Serve America Act will increase the size of AmeriCorps from 75,000 volunteers to 250,000 by 2017.
- The Act also creates a Social Innovation Fund that will invest in ideas that are proven to improve outcomes and "what works" funds in federal agencies to promote effective and innovative programs.
- The American Recovery and Reinvestment Act included $201 million in funding for the Corporation for National and Community Service to support an expansion of AmeriCorps State and National and AmeriCorps VISTA programs.

### *Guiding Principles*

President Obama has always been a strong supporter of empowering ordinary people to do extraordinary things by improving their local communities through service. President Obama asks how we—through both existing organizations and individual action—can take an active role in America's economic recovery and improve our fellow citizens' lives through our service work.

## Promote Sustained Civic Engagement

President Obama believes that service consists of more than a "one-off" occasion. He believes that civic engagement and service should be a lifelong commitment whether at the school, community, city, state, or national level. This includes community service, government service, and military service. By empowering people at all stages of their lives and at all levels of society to stand up and help solve problems in their own communities, the federal government will encourage sustained civic engagement that will transform those serving, the communities they help, and the nation as a whole.

## Measure Results

President Obama believes in measuring the outcomes of service—not just the hours served or number of volunteers—to enhance what works and avoid using resources on ineffective programs. He will encourage planning, goal-setting, and execution by volunteers at the local level, so that volunteering is tied into a united and measured effort across the nation.

## Reward Innovative Solutions to Pressing Social Problems

President Obama envisions a social innovation framework for the 21st century that reflects a new social contract: citizens actively and effectively serving their communities, solving problems, and connecting their service to a larger effort. Government will serve as an innovative, efficient, transparent, and accountable catalyst for service. The President will expand service opportunities to enable all Americans to enlist in an effort to meet the nation's challenges and will leverage investments in the nonprofit sector—a critical problem-solving partner and social innovation engine. He will also promote innovations within government by seeking out what works in federal programs and expanding best practices.

From White House, www.whitehouse.gov/issues/service/. Accessed on February 1, 2010.

## Asking Clarification Questions

Read the statements from the reading on pages 10–11. Imagine you had questions about these views for a candidate running for office. Write clarification questions.

1. He believes that civic engagement and service should be a lifelong commitment whether at the school, community, city, state, or national level.

*I think that civic engagement and service is very important, if he did this, a lot of civilse will support him.*

2. By empowering people at all stages of their lives and at all levels of society to stand up and help solve problems in their own communities, the federal government will encourage sustained civic engagement that will transform those serving, the communities they help, and the nation as a whole.

*It's necessary to do like that, but I think it's not enough, education system and safety are also important.*

3. He will encourage planning, goal-setting, and execution by volunteers at the local level, so that volunteering is tied into a united and measured effort across the nation.

*Civils' suggestions is very important, it's good for government's work.*

4. Government will serve as an innovative, efficient, transparent, and accountable catalyst for service.

*Government's service should be better, innovative service is the most important.*

5. The President will expand service opportunities to enable all Americans to enlist in an effort to meet the nation's challenges and will leverage investments in the nonprofit sector—a critical problem-solving partner and social innovation engine.

*It can decrease civils pressure.*

6. He will also promote innovations within government by seeking out what works in federal programs and expanding best practices.

*Innovations is one of the most important part of government, it should be better.*

Work with a partner. Person A should read the original statement. Person B should ask the clarification question. Then Person A can give clarification using one of the phrases on page 6. Take turns.

## Strategy: Listening for and Using Contractions

In conversations, academic discussions, and even in formal lectures, native English speakers use contractions. Even though some contractions are grammatically correct, this contracted English is generally considered less formal.

A contraction is shortening two words into one by omitting letters and inserting an apostrophe (').

Many contractions form the negative—by using the word *not*.

> is not = *isn't*
>
> are not = *aren't*

Other contractions are formed using pronouns and auxiliary verbs.

> she will = *she'll*
>
> would have = *would've*

Some contractions are considered very informal and are used primarily in spoken English.

> here is = *here's*
>
> what is = *what's*
>
> that will = *that'll*
>
> who would = *who'd*

## Practicing Contractions

Combine these words into commonly used contractions in English.

1. I am _I'm_
2. he will _he'll_
3. we have _We've_
4. you are _You're_
5. they had _they'd_
6. need not _needn't_
7. what will _what'll_

Write these contractions in more formal, non-contracted English.

8. I've _I have_
9. it's _It is_
10. we're _We are_
11. you'll _you will_
12. they've _they have_
13. oughtn't _ought not_
14. what's _what is_

## Practicing More Formal English

Cross out the contraction, and write the more formal English on the line. Then read the sentences aloud both ways to a partner. Discuss which you like better.

1. He's a political candidate but hasn't won the election yet so he's not an office holder.

   _____

2. I'd taken the entrance examination the July before. It's required for admittance to the school of political science.

   _____

3. I didn't know a thing about the voting system, but I was determined to learn so I'd be able to work for the government.

   _____

4. I wasn't out there to waste time; I wanted to work on a presidential campaign, and I wouldn't give up my dream.

   _____

5. I could've done something else, but I chose to keep studying. They'd accept me into the school's program after my test scores were recorded.

   _____

6. She's great. If you're writing a campaign speech and need help, she'll be there for you. If you're struggling with ideas, then she'll show up to offer her ideas.

   _____

7. They're the voters that'll make the final decision, so don't say the wrong things.

   _____

## Speaking

### Agreeing and Disagreeing

In conversations and group discussions, you have to agree and disagree with what someone else is saying. Most people think it is easier to agree, but sometimes you have to disagree. When you agree and disagree, your choice of phrase and your tone of voice are important. Consider who you are talking with and what you are talking about when choosing the best words and tone to use.

FORMAL AGREEING AND DISAGREEING

| Agreeing |
|---|
| *That's a good point.* |
| *I agree with you.* |
| *That's what I think, too.* |
| *I share your opinion.* |
| *You're correct.* |
| *I'm in complete agreement with you.* |

| Disagreeing |
|---|
| *I don't think so.* |
| *I don't agree.* |
| *I'm afraid I disagree with what you're saying.* |
| *I'm sorry, but I don't share your opinion.* |
| *That's not the way I see it.* |

INFORMAL AGREEING AND DISAGREEING

| Agreeing |
|---|
| *You bet!* |
| *You can say that again.* |
| *No doubt!* |
| *Right.* |

| Disagreeing |
|---|
| *Are you kidding?* |
| *You're not serious, are you?* |
| *No way.* |
| *You're crazy.* |

A good strategy to use is to acknowledge the other person's opinion before stating your opposite opinion. Some phrases you can use to acknowledge others' opinions first <u>before</u> you say what you think are:

ACKNOWLEDGING BEFORE DISAGREEING

| |
|---|
| *I see what you're saying, but I believe . . .* |
| *I understand your point, but I don't completely agree with you on . . .* |
| *You are entitled to your opinion, but I think . . .* |
| *I respect your idea, but don't you also think . . .* |
| *I don't like disagreeing, but in my opinion . . .* |

ASKING ABOUT AGREEMENT OR DISAGREEMENT

| |
|---|
| *Do you agree?* |
| *Don't you agree?* |
| *What do you think?* |
| *How do you feel?* |
| *Would you agree or disagree?* |

## Role-Playing

Work with two classmates to role play possible conversations for these situations. Use the phrases in the boxes on pages 16–17 or others that you can think of to write dialogues. Then exchange roles. Read your dialogues to the class.

### SITUATIONS

the school's biggest problem

the country's best strategy to overcome poverty

the best way to save money

the biggest economic obstacle facing the world

Person A begins by stating an idea about the situation.

Person B will agree or disagree and ask Person C about agreement.

Person C will agree with Person A or B.

Person A:

_____

Person B:

_____

Person A:

_____

Person C:

_____

Can you extend the conversations with other ideas, agreements, and disagreements?

_____

_____

_____

_____

_____

## Listening 2: Talking about Issues

### Listening in Groups

Listen to the students discuss the candidates running for mayor. Discuss the questions in a small group.

**Focus on Language**

1. List any contractions that you heard. Did any of the contractions make the conversation difficult to understand? Do you think there were too many or two few?

   *doesn't he's what's it's let's*     NO   Too few

2. What phrases are used to express agreement? Note: Don't worry about writing exact words.

   support it . imp. I like/ two plctn

3. What phrases are used to express disagreement? Note: Don't worry about writing exact words.

   right?   No way ,   instead   Really?   it's not different   Don't you think. but how

4. Write any phrases or idioms that you are not familiar with. Discuss what they mean and in what type of interactions they are appropriate.

   qualified   comprehensive . campaign

**Focus on Tone**

1. The word *but* is used several times throughout the interaction. What does the tone indicate about the person's level of agreement to the opinion it follows? Why do you think the word *but* is used so frequently?

   <u>Someone **so** say "but" lightly is about be agreement.</u>
   <u>Because "but" is a basic word.</u>

2. Describe the tone used by each member of the group.

   <u>the boy is confident.</u>

3. One student discusses hospitals and parks. What are her feelings about the candidate and issues? One student discusses crime. What are his feelings about the candidate and the issue? Another student discusses education. What are her feelings about the candidate and the issue? How can you tell?

   <u>① **As the** more experience, house care, city manage,</u>
   <u>② environment, public safety, department ③. school's budget is important.</u>
   <u>Education system</u>

**Focus on Nonverbal Communication**

1. What nonverbal cues are used to show agreement?

   <u>body language, nodding, shrug her shoulders</u>

2. What nonverbal cues are used to show disagreement?

   <u>body language, shake her head. knit his brows</u>

3. Which student do you think has the most expressive facial expressions? Does this positively or negatively affect the interaction?

   <u>This boy. Positively.</u>

## Summary

1. How strongly do you think the speakers feel about their opinions? What evidence is there to support your opinion?

   I suppose that public safety and education system are the most important. Because education and safety are the basic requirement of a country.

2. Who would you most want to work with on a political campaign? Why?

   The first people, because his father works for government, so he can have experience about government's work. And he advocates @ environment and public safety, these are very important

3. Is there anyone you would want to avoid working with? Why?

   No, because all of these persons have their points, and everyone has advantages, so I think I want to work with each other.

**You Be the Judge**

One issue that many politicians disagree on is capital punishment—the death penalty or execution; a person who committed a crime should be put to death by the government. In some countries, the death penalty has been abolished. In others, it is still an acceptable punishment. In the United States, the governor of a state can reduce or eliminate the death penalty. In other words, he or she can grant clemency, or forgiveness, even if a judge has sentenced someone to death.

Read this court case about a death penalty punishment.

---

In 1982, a young mother of three was murdered in her apartment in Virginia. Almost a year later, a 22-year-old man was arrested for burglary and malicious wounding in a nearby county. He was questioned for two days, and police said he confessed to several crimes, including the young mother's murder. The man had a general IQ of about 69 (an average intelligence quotient is considered 100) and gave inconsistent answers when being questioned by the police. For example, he testified that the murder victim was short when in fact she was tall. His confession and his identification of a shirt given to the police led to his death penalty. He was also sentenced to prison for the burglary and malicious wounding charges. The young man appealed, but failed, and his execution date drew closer.

The man's case was taken on by a law firm in New York. The attorneys secured a stay of execution for him only nine days before his execution date. After that, an appeals court ruled that it was true the man received ineffective assistance of counsel at his trial since not all of the biological evidence was introduced, but he was still guilty because of his confessions. DNA testing was conducted, and it released him from guilt in the murder. However, the Virginia General Assembly rejected legislation that would have given the man a new trial. Too much time had passed. The law had spoken.

---

1. If you were the governor of Virginia, would you grant clemency to the man?
   Write two or three reasons for your decision.

   _____

   _____

   _____

   _____

2. Would you consider the charges for the burglary and malicious wounding in
   your decision? Write two or three reasons for your decision.

   _____

   _____

   _____

   _____

3. Work with a small group. Discuss your decisions and your reasons. Come to
   a group consensus. What did you decide? Present your decisions to the rest of
   the class.

   _____

   _____

   _____

   _____

# Part 3: Elections

## Pre-Listening Activities

An election is a process by which people decide who will lead the group, organization, or government. The selection of the person or persons is deliberately made by the population of the club, business, or city, state, or country he or she will represent. Government elections differ based on country and type of government. Answer these questions with a partner.

1. What is voting like in a country you are familiar with? Discuss the process, rules, and characteristics of elections.

   _____

   _____

   _____

2. Have you ever voted? What was the experience like?

   _____

   _____

   _____

3. What characteristics do you think someone needs to be an effective leader of a country?

   _____

   _____

   _____

## Strategy: Listening for and Using Signal Words and Phrases

Speakers often use signal words to let you know when a comparison or contrast or an example is going to follow.

### Words or Phrases that Signal Contrasting Ideas

*on the other hand*

> The direct election system has advantages. On the other hand, direct elections can have drawbacks.

*on the contrary*

> In direct elections, voters cast their ballots directly for the person they want to win. On the contrary, in indirect elections, voters select other people who will then make the selection.

*to contrast* or *in contrast*

> In Algeria, voters directly choose the person they want to be the head of state. In contrast, citizens of the United States indirectly vote for the head of state.

*unlike* or *contrarily*

> Unlike Algeria, the United States has an indirect election for the head of state.

### Words or Phrases that Signal Similar Ideas

*likewise*

> Some Asian countries have direct elections. Likewise, several European nations hold them, too.

*similarly*

> Taiwan holds a direct election to elect its president; similarly, France holds a direct election for its head of state.

*also*

> Some countries use both direct and indirect elections. France holds a direct election for its presidential race, but uses an indirect election for some other offices. Also, the United States uses a combination of election types.

*in addition*

> In addition, the nation of Gabon, in Africa, has a combination of elections like France.

## Words or Phrases that Signal Examples

*for example*

> Some Asian countries have direct elections. For example, Taiwan holds a direct election for the head of state and for other offices.

*for instance*

> Other Asian countries don't have an election system at all when choosing the head of state; for instance, Japan has a monarchy.

*to illustrate*

> Some countries have one type of election for all offices. To illustrate this, think about Ghana.

*to show*

> To show how indirect elections work, I'm going to discuss the presidential election in the United States.

## Using Signal Words

Write a sentence or pair of sentences on any topic using the country and the signal word or phrase given. One has been done for you as an example.

1. United States / likewise

   *The summer months in the United States are June, July, and August.*

   *Likewise, Canada's summer also begins in June.*

2. Germany / similarly

   There are ~~Germany have~~ good car industry *in Germany* Similarly Intiliy also have good car industry

3. People's Republic of China / in contrast

   There are (1,300,000) People's republic of chin

4. Brazil / unlike

5. Australia / for instance

6. Nigeria / to illustrate

## Note-Taking

### Strategy: Using Venn Diagrams to Show Relationships

A Venn diagram is a graphic organizer made up of two or more interconnecting circles. The circles show relationships between ideas and provide a visual representation of notes. When a lecture has a lot of information comparing and contrasting two things, it is a good idea to move the notes into a Venn diagram to help create a picture and organize the examples.

**Steps**

1. Write notes as your instructor lectures. Look at your lecture notes and think about the concepts the instructor talked about.

2. List the characteristics, examples, and other notes for each concept.

3. Draw a Venn diagram with enough space to write.

4. In the area to the left, write characteristics or examples of one concept.

5. In the area to the right, write the characteristics or examples of the other.

6. In the overlapping area, write the characteristics or examples they share.

You'll have the chance to complete a blank Venn diagram when you listen to the next lecture (see page 32). If used correctly, you'll be able to answer some questions about the main idea and details from the lecture.

## Completing a Venn Diagram

Work with a partner. Complete the Venn diagram with words to describe your native country and its leader on the left and your partner's on the right. Put words that describe both in the middle. Then write sentences using signal words to compare, contrast, and give examples.

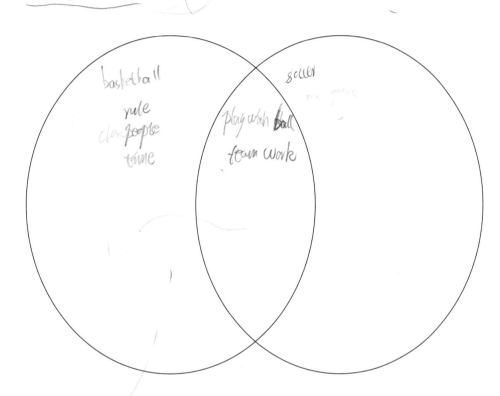

1. Write two sentences using comparison signals.

   _____

   _____

2. Write two sentences using contrast signals.

   _____

   _____

3. Write two sentences using example signals.

   _____

   _____

**Vocabulary Power**

There are a number of terms and phrases in this lecture that you may encounter in other academic settings. Add at least five vocabulary items to your vocabulary notebook or log.

Match the words in bold from the lecture on the left with a definition on the right.

1. __C__ . . . for instance, have a direct election when selecting its head of state, and then **employ** an indirect election process for other offices.

2. __e__ In other words, they choose, and their vote is counted as one for that **particular** person.

3. __g__ It's a challenging concept to **wrap your mind around**, isn't it?

4. __a__ In addition to the U.S., Switzerland, Germany, and Italy also select heads of states **via** the process of indirect elections.

5. __h__ Those **tend** to prefer an indirect system.

6. __b__ Every hand a politician shakes could lead to a direct vote and **propel** him or her into office.

7. __d__ Historically, the number of electoral votes and the popular—or **majority** vote—was in favor of the same candidate.

8. __f__ . . . and Al Gore, having more of the **popular** vote.

a. by way of

b. move

c. use

d. greater number

e. specific

f. general people's

g. understand

h. seem

## Listening 3: Elections

### Listening to a Lecture

The listening passage is a lecture from a political science class. The instructor is discussing two types of elections: direct and indirect. Throughout the lecture, the instructor compares and contrasts the two types of elections and gives many examples. Use the Venn diagram to organize your notes after you listen to the lecture on direct and indirect elections. Fill in the Venn diagram with characteristics and examples of each type of election. Follow the process listed in the box on page 28.

Step 1: Write notes.

Same country          relaxtus

                          Gan a

         -      - policys

         accidence

Now    stay offices
                    derect  apaulin

         party
    discount    particulas  person

 most  common  system        primary  system

   of Canana    Africa  peoney   America  Mexica
        one way      people  citizens

         of  Group  people
              USA          voting  from  Canada

         USA  Swhodland  Germany  Italy  Lnderspction voting

  In Japan   -    more  people,  papulay  in  majority
         United States ,  presidens  -  different  4  year  or  8 years

Step 2: List the characteristics, examples, and other notes of each concept.

| Direct Elections | Indirect Elections |
|---|---|
|  |  |
|  |  |
|  |  |
|  |  |
|  |  |
|  |  |
|  |  |
|  |  |

Steps 3–6: Complete the Venn diagram.

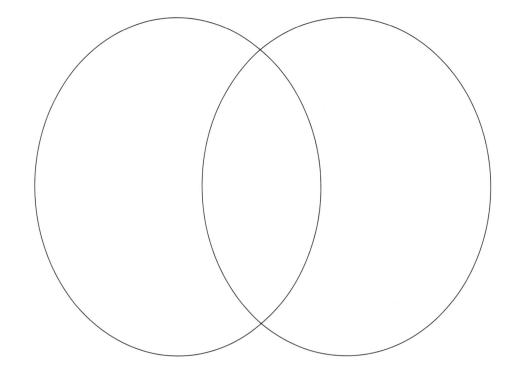

## Checking Your Understanding: Main Ideas

Review your notes. Listen again to the lecture if necessary, and then put a check mark (✓) next to the statements that best reflect the main ideas.

1. _____ An election for a country's head of state can be both direct and indirect.

2. ✓ In both types of elections, citizens get to vote.

3. ✓ Voters in a direct election have their vote counted for the candidate.

4. ✓ Voters in an indirect election have their vote counted for an elector.

5. _____ The popular vote and the electoral vote are the same thing.

## Checking Your Understanding: Details

Use your Venn diagram, and put a check mark (✓) next to the best answers. Some questions have more than one answer.

1. Which of these countries use a direct election to select its head of state?

   a. ✓ Indonesia

   b. ✓ Mexico

   c. _____ United States

   d. _____ Italy

2. Which of these countries use an indirect election to select its head of state?

   a. ✓ Switzerland

   b. _____ Kenya

   c. ✓ Germany

   d. _____ Ghana

3. Which of these organizations more often use a direct election to select their leaders?

    a. _____ schools

    b. _✓_ clubs

    c. _____ unions

    d. _____ workplace organizations

4. Which of these organizations prefer to use an indirect election to select their leaders?

    a. _____ schools

    b. _____ clubs

    c. _✓_ unions

    d. _✓_ workplace organizations

## Debate

In a debate, teams of speakers discuss the positive points (called the **pros**) and the negative points (called the **cons**) of a topic or issue. Debating well does not depend on whether or not you actually agree with the issue. Good debating has to do with your speaking, listening, and critical thinking skills. Can you listen to the other team's argument? Can you react quickly? Can you disagree and counter?

Divide the class into two teams, and study the list of issues commonly discussed by presidential candidates in the United States. The class will vote to debate one topic. One team will argue in support of the issue; the other will argue against (or rebut) the issue.

| | |
|---|---|
| the death penalty | health care for all citizens |
| education | a higher minimum wage |
| foreign policy | immigration |
| gun control | taxes |

Topic: _____

Pro or Con: _____

Choose one team member to give an introductory statement and one to give a closing statement. Divide the arguments evenly among the remaining team members. Be prepared to disagree and counter at least one point from the other team. Each statement, argument, and counterargument lasts for two minutes.

Follow this debate format:

> Pro team member gives an introductory statement on the topic to present/preview pro opinion
>
> Con team gives an introductory statement on the topic to present/preview con opinion
>
> Con team member delivers first argument
>
> Pro team member rebuts with counterargument
>
> Pro team member delivers next argument
>
> Con team member rebuts with counterargument
>
> Team members will continue exchanging arguments and rebuttals until all team members have delivered their arguments and counterarguments.
>
> Open discussion (10 minutes)
>
> Pro team member gives a closing statement/summary on pro team's argument
>
> Con team member gives a closing statement/summary on con team's argument

Team member giving introductory statement _____

Team member giving closing statement _____

Other arguments: _____

_____

_____

_____

_____

**Preparing Individually**

Think about the selected topic, and then write two reasons that support the issue and two that are against the issue. You need to think about both sides so that you can argue effectively against the other team.

Pro 1:

_____

_____

_____

Pro 2:

_____

_____

_____

Con 1:

_____

_____

_____

Con 2:

_____

_____

_____

**Preparing as a Group**

Now work with your team. Take turns discussing your pros and cons. Your group should select the strongest pros and cons to use during the debate. Select arguments that you think will be difficult for the other team to disagree with. Also think about responses you can use to counter the other team's arguments.

Arguments:

_____

_____

_____

_____

_____

_____

_____

_____

Counterarguments:

_____

_____

_____

_____

_____

_____

_____

_____

# Rapid Vocabulary Review

From the three answers on the right, circle the one that best explains, is an example of, or combines with the vocabulary item on the left as it is used in this unit.

| Vocabulary | Answers | | |
|---|---|---|---|
| Synonyms | | | |
| 1. platform | systems | policies | designs |
| 2. poverty | percentage | participation | neediness |
| 3. on the other hand | similar to | in contrast | approximately |
| 4. kidding | joking | seeming | tending |
| 5. majority | less than 1% | more than 50% | almost 100% |
| 6. viewpoints | hopes | opinions | jobs |
| 7. seek | look for | listen to | put off |
| 8. ideal | likely | possible | perfect |
| 9. instances | quick motions | memories | examples |
| 10. superior | worse than | better than | equal to |
| 11. encourage | improve | urge | move |
| 12. deliberately | automatically | convincingly | intentionally |
| Combinations and Associations | | | |
| 13. to overcome ____ | an obstacle | information | a link |
| 14. comprised ____ | in | of | with |
| 15. focus ____ | on | at | in |
| 16. pros and ____ | negatives | cons | disadvantages |
| 17. solve ____ | a problem | an event | a judgment |
| 18. ____ the contrary | at | in | on |
| 19. entitled ____ | by | for | to |
| 20. ____ all | after | before | since |

# ⇨✕⊐ Synthesizing: Projects and Presentations

| Short In-Class Speaking Assignments | Longer Outside Assignments |
|---|---|
| A Good Leader | Electing a Leader |
| Who do you think has been an influential leader? This person can be anyone that you feel has made a mark on the world or on you personally. State who you choose and why you think that person is a good leader. | Work with a group to start a new nation. Imagine you are the electors responsible for choosing the leader of your nation. Create the ideal candidate. Consider physical attributes, experience, family, educational background, and emotional and mental qualities. Prepare a short presentation describing your candidate, his or her views on major issues. Be prepared to clarify or offer more details after questions and disagreement from the nation's population (your classmates). |
| Nominations | Delivering a Campaign Speech |
| What famous person would you want to run your school? Why? State the person you'd choose and state what you think he or she could do for the school. | Watch campaign speeches that you find on websites, television, or videos. With your group, write a campaign speech for your candidate and then divide the speech into sections so each member will present one part of the speech. Use signals as appropriate. |

## Vocabulary Log

To increase your vocabulary knowledge, write a definition or translation for each vocabulary item. Then write an original phrase, sentence, or note that will help you remember the vocabulary item.

| Vocabulary Item | Definition or Translation | Your Original Phrase, Sentence, or Note |
|---|---|---|
| 1. accomplish | to complete (something) | I didn't accomplish much yesterday. |
| 2. exchange | substitute | _____ one thing for another |
| 3. evenly | equally | _____ divided |
| 4. legislation | | |
| 5. envision | | |
| 6. mere | | |
| 7. to shift | | |
| 8. to clarify | | |
| 9. roles | | |
| 10. a format | | |
| 11. to face | | |
| 12. to abolish | | |
| 13. murder | | |
| 14. arrest | | |

| Vocabulary Item | Definition or Translation | Your Original Phrase, Sentence, or Note |
|---|---|---|
| 15. a burglary | | |
| 16. IQ | | |
| 17. to confess | | |
| 18. to testify | | |
| 19. a penalty | | |
| 20. to sentence | | |
| 21. to reject | | |
| 22. comprehensive | | |
| 23. essentially | | |
| 24. entitled to | | |
| 25. mental | | |

# 2 Health: Nutrition

Health is not only being free from sickness. In general, health is the state of being well physically and mentally. One facet of health studies is nutrition—the scientific study of foods and diet and how they are used by the body. This unit focuses on types of foods and how they affect a person's overall health.

# Part 1: Fast Food

## Pre-Listening Activities

Even though fast food isn't the healthiest food choice, people are choosing to eat it in record numbers. Fast food is often inexpensive and prepared and served with little wait time for the customer. Some people say that saving time often sacrifices quality or nutritional value. Fast food establishments used to primarily serve hamburgers, but now you can find restaurants serving chicken, pizza, or tacos. Answer these questions with a partner.

1.  How frequently do you visit fast food establishments? What are your favorite fast food restaurants and menu items?

    _____

    _____

    _____

2.  Do you think people are aware of the negative characteristics of fast food? Why do you think people choose to eat fast food even though the calorie and fat gram counts are high and other nutritional values are low?

    _____

    _____

    _____

3. Normally active women need to consume about 1,800 calories per day
   while normally active men need 2,200 calories per day. Read the foods
   in the first column. In the second column, rank the food by how many
   calories it has. Write 1 for the food that you think has the most calories,
   2 for the next highest, and on through 10 for the item with the fewest
   calories. What did you consider in your ranking of the items?

   _____

   _____

   _____

**CALORIES IN FAST FOOD ITEMS**

| Food Item | Your Ranking Guess |
|---|---|
| Cheeseburger | |
| Chicken sandwich | |
| Cola drink (large) | |
| Fish sandwich (with tartar sauce and cheese) | |
| French fries (large) | |
| Fried chicken (drumstick) | |
| Hamburger (plain) | |
| Hot fudge sundae | |
| Pepperoni pizza (1/8 slice) | |
| Taco (with meat and cheese) | |

## Strategy: Listening for and Giving Ordinal Numerical Information

Speakers use a lot of numbers both to provide information and supply rankings.

Ordinal numbers are used to describe an item's place or position in an order or sequence. The ranking could refer to chronology, importance, or size.

> the fourth step
>
> the third most populous country
>
> the second tallest

Ordinals are also used when giving dates.

> January 29th
>
> the 8th of June

Therefore, if you hear an ordinal number, you already have an idea what the speaker is talking about.

The first three ordinals are the most difficult to remember because they don't sound like their cardinal or whole number. Most of the time, ordinal numbers sound like the cardinal or whole number with a –th sound added.

| Cardinal number | Ordinal number |
|:---:|:---|
| 1 | first |
| 2 | second |
| 3 | third |

Note that whenever 1, 2, or 3 is used as part of an ordinal, the ending remains the same.

| | |
|:---:|:---|
| 21 | twenty-first |
| 22 | twenty-second |
| 23 | twenty-third |

The other ordinals add a –th ending and often you can hear the name of the cardinal number when you say the ordinal.

*Pronunciation Note*: There are two –th sounds, one that uses your voice and one that uses your breath. The –th in ordinal numbers uses breath. To make the sound, put your tongue between your teeth and blow a puff of air out. You should not use your vocal cords to make this sound.

| Cardinal | Ordinal |
|---|---|
| 4 | fourth |
| 5 | fifth |
| 6 | sixth |
| 7 | seventh |
| 8 | eighth |
| 9 | ninth |
| 10 | tenth |
| 11 | eleventh |
| 12 | twelfth |
| 13 | thirteenth |
| 14 | fourteenth |
| 15 | fifteenth |
| 16 | sixteenth |
| 17 | seventeenth |
| 18 | eighteenth |
| 19 | nineteenth |

From here, you can convert any number into an ordinal.

| | |
|---|---|
| 27 | twenty-seventh |
| 42 | forty-second |
| 88 | eighty-eight |
| 100 | one hundredth |

## Practicing Ordinal Numbers

Write five phrases using ordinal numbers. Say them to a partner, expressing yourself clearly in English. Then change roles.

| Your Phrases | Your Partner's Phrases |
|---|---|
|  |  |
|  |  |
|  |  |
|  |  |
|  |  |

## Listening 1: An Informational Seminar

### Listening for Information

The listening passage is an excerpt from a seminar given at a student health center. The seminar is an informational meeting on the calories in common fast food items. Write your ranking guesses from page 45 in the last column. As you listen to the informational seminar on the audio, fill in the second and third columns of the chart.

CALORIES IN FAST FOOD ITEMS

| Food Item | Calories | Ranking (1 = most calories) | Your Ranking Guess |
|---|---|---|---|
| Cheeseburger | | | |
| Chicken sandwich | | | |
| Cola drink (large) | | | |
| Fish sandwich (with tartar sauce and cheese) | | | |
| French fries (large) | | | |
| Fried chicken (drumstick) | | | |
| Hamburger (plain) | | | |
| Hot fudge sundae | | | |
| Pepperoni pizza (1/8 slice) | | | |
| Taco (with meat and cheese) | | | |

## Speaking

### Expressing Likes and Dislikes

When you talk about preferences, there are certain phrases you can use to express what you like and what you don't. Always consider who you are talking to and what you are talking about. In formal or academic settings, strong phrases might not be appropriate even if you really love or hate something. You may choose weaker statements to avoid hurting someone's feelings.

| Expressing Likes | Expressing Dislikes |
| --- | --- |
| *I like. . .* | *I don't like/dislike. . .* |
| *I really like. . .* | *I really don't like. . .* |
| *I'm happy with/about. . .* | *I'm unhappy with/about. . .* |
| *I'm satisfied. . .* | *I'm disappointed. . .* |
| *I'm content. . .* | *I can't tolerate. . .* |
| *This is great. . .* | *This is terrible. . .* |
| *I love. . .* | *I hate. . .* |

Which phrases do you think are the strongest? What other adjectives can you think of to express likes and dislikes?

_____

_____

_____

_____

**Discussing**

Use the chart on page 48 to answer these questions with a partner.

1.  How many did you get correct? Which ones? Discuss why your rankings were incorrect.

    _____

    _____

    _____

2.  Which rankings surprised you the most? Which surprised you the least?

    _____

    _____

    _____

3.  Do the numbers make you think more about what you will order next time you eat at a fast food restaurant? Why or why not? Which items would be easy for you to give up? Which would be more difficult to stop eating?

    _____

    _____

    _____

## Analyzing the Situation

Work with a partner. Read each situation, and decide what you would say or do to express your feelings. Use *like* or *dislike* appropriately. Write a dialogue for each on a separate piece of paper.

1. Last week the teaching assistant wrote math problems on the board to help explain the content and that was helpful. This week he is only walking you through the textbook and you're not learning as much.

   _____

   _____

2. The student body president is holding a meeting to get feedback on the university's plan to raise tuition. You already have to work at the cafeteria to help pay for tuition. You can't afford to pay an increase in your tuition.

   _____

   _____

3. One of your instructors offers to hold an extra study group session to help prepare for the final exam. You'd prefer to get some one-on-one help.

   _____

   _____

## Making an Impromptu Speech

When it is your turn, your teacher will randomly select one of these topics. You will have two minutes to answer the question by stating your preference and why you like it and dislike other options.

Topic 1: What's the best way to lose weight: change your eating habits or exercise more?

Topic 2: What's the best type of fast food: hamburgers, tacos, or pizza?

Topic 3: What's the best type of fast food: chicken, fish, or fries?

Topic 4: Which diet is more successful: one that counts calories or one that is liquid only?

Topic 5: Which do you prefer: meat or vegetables?

Topic 6: Which do you prefer for dessert: ice cream, cake, or pie?

Topic 7: What kind of food do you prefer: American, Chinese, or Mexican?

Topic 8: What kind of food do you prefer: French, Italian, or German?

## Part 2: Discussing Pros and Cons

### Pre-Listening Activities

For most people, deciding what to eat and drink is a normal part of everyday life. They make decisions about what to eat to provide nutrition and hydration to their bodies. Unfortunately, some people suffer from mental or physical problems that prevent them from making such decisions. Answer these questions with a partner.

1. What does the word *artificial* mean? What are some foods and drinks that are artificial?

   _____

   _____

   _____

2. If you were unable to make decisions about your health, who would you want to make them for you? Why?

   _____

   _____

   _____

3. What have you heard about artificial nutrition and hydration?

   _____

   _____

   _____

This section discusses a sensitive topic: artificial nutrition. Artificial nutrition is a method used to sustain life when people are unable to feed themselves or make the decision to eat at all. Artificial nutrition is a mix of nutrients and liquids that are given to the person via a tube. A medical professional must administer and withdraw the artificial means of nutrition, but sometimes a person's family can make the decision about continuing the treatment.

## Strategy: Listening for Reductions and Ellipses

In many conversations, native speakers shorten or eliminate sounds and words from their speech. The deletion of sounds is called a **reduction;** the deletion of words is called an **ellipsis.** Words that are usually reduced are function words—small words that don't carry as much meaning, such as prepositions, articles, and pronouns. Because they don't carry as much meaning, don't worry if you miss them when listening. The best thing to do is become familiar with common reductions in English. Some reductions are written with an apostrophe to indicate that letters have been deleted.

### Common Reductions

*didya* = did you
Didya study for the test yet?

*howbout* = how about
Howbout we meet at the library to study?

*'im, 'er, 'is* = him, her, his
I gave 'im is book back so he could give it to 'er before she goes to eat.

*wanna* = want to
I wanna study for the health exam. *Howbout* we go tomorrow instead?

*gonna* = going to
John's gonna take the nutrition class because he wants to be a doctor.

*oughta* = ought to
Jane oughta take that class because she wants to be a nurse.

*hafta, hasta, hada* = have to, has to, had to
They're both gonna hafta study a lot. Anyone hasta study a lot to work in the medical field.

*n* = and
Mike said 'is advisor told 'im to take nutrition 'n biology to prep for medical school.

Words that are usually shortened or completely left out in natural English are usually main subjects (nouns), main verbs, and helping verbs. Even though it is grammatical to have these important parts of speech, spoken English is more relaxed. Even with the deletions, the content can usually be understood.

### Sample Ellipses with Reductions

*Whatcha think about a pizza?* = What do you think about ordering/having a pizza?

*Howbout a person with Alzheimer's?* = What is your opinion about a person suffering from Alzheimer's?

## Practing Eliminating Reductions

Translate these sentences from how they might sound in spoken English to how they would be written.

1. Howbout goin' to 'is study session Thursday night?

   How about going to his study session Thursday night?

2. Ya gotta think 'bout people in comas. Doctors should help 'em.

   _____

   _____

3. Wanna go over this material again? We hafta study the online notes 'n the textbook chapter.

   _____

   _____

4. The teacher assistant tol' me that the teacher writes 'is tests from information in the textbook so we need ta study the chapter.

   _____

   _____

5. We've studied so much. I hafta get some sleep. Gotta go. See ya in the mornin'.

   _____

   _____

## Speaking

### Discussing Pros and Cons

In academic conversations and group discussions, you will have to discuss two sides of issues. A good strategy is to offer a pro argument and then a con argument in your statements. A transition word or phrase can be used to connect the two. If someone else makes a positive or negative statement, then you can use a transition and offer the opposing view.

**COMMON TRANSITIONS**

| | | |
|---|---|---|
| *although* | *even so / though* | *regardless* |
| *but* | *in spite of* | *still* |
| *however* | *nevertheless* | *yet* |

**POSING THE NEGATIVE (CON)**

When someone offers a positive statement, another person may point out the negative after a transition.

Person 1:
She has a great resume.

Person 2:
*Regardless*, it's a tough economy and it could be hard to find a job.

Person 1:
Now is a good time to study nursing. In a few years there will be a nursing shortage, and it'll be easier to find a job.

Person 2:
*However,* with the economy suffering as it is, hospitals are not getting the same funding they used to. In that case, they might not be able to hire new nurses even if they're needed.

**POSING THE POSITIVE (PRO)**

Note that the negative argument can be delivered first. The alternate formula is adding a transition word or phrase, and then giving a positive statement.

Person 1:
That topic is going to require a lot of research and time.

Person 2:
*Still,* it's a good choice because it's creative. We'll probably get a better grade.

## Practicing Pros and Cons

Work with a partner. Person A should make a positive statement about one of the topics. Person B should then choose a transition and add a negative statement. Then exchange roles.

Example: fast food

Person A:
I am happy there is a McDonald's on campus because it's fast and convenient. I have time to grab a burger between classes.

Person B:
Even so, I'd rather take more time to go to the deli at the student union because it offers healthier options.

Topics:

| | |
|---|---|
| fast food | healthy food options |
| favorite foods | meal plan options |
| health classes | restaurants in town |

Can you extend the conversation with other ideas and phrases from Unit 1?

_____

_____

_____

_____

_____

Write a few of your statements. Are there any words or phrases that a native speaker would reduce or ellipse? Practice reading them.

_____

_____

_____

_____

_____

# Listening 2: Discussing Pros and Cons

## Listening in Groups

Listen to the students discuss the topic of artificial nutrition covered in their nutrition class. Discuss the questions in a small group.

## Focus on Language

1. What phrases of like and dislike are used? Which ones are stronger? Which ones sound weaker? <u>Note</u>: Don't worry about writing exact words?

   _____

   _____

2. What transitions are used to connect pro and con arguments?

   _____

   _____

3. List instances of reductions or ellipses that you noticed. Do any of them make the conversation difficult to follow?

   _____

   _____

4. Write any phrases or idioms that you are not familiar with. Discuss what they mean and in what type of interactions they are appropriate.

   _____

   _____

## Focus on Tone

1. Describe the tone used by each member of the group.

   _____

   _____

2. Two students discuss a religious aspect to artificial nutrition. What can you
   tell about their feelings from their tone?

   _____

   _____

3. Is each person's tone appropriate? Why or why not?

   _____

   _____

## Focus on Nonverbal Communication

1. What nonverbal cues are used to show how each member of the group feels?

   _____

   _____

2. In your opinion, are any of these inappropriate? Why or why not?

   _____

   _____

3. Which student do you think has the most expressive facial expressions? Does
   this positively or negatively affect the interaction?

   _____

   _____

## Summary

1. Who do you think represented himself or herself the best during the interaction? What language, tone, and nonverbal evidence can you use to support your choice?

_____

_____

_____

_____

2. Who would you most want to talk about something serious with? Why?

_____

_____

_____

_____

3. Is there anyone you would want to avoid working with? Why?

_____

_____

_____

_____

**You Be the Judge**

Sometimes people disagree about a family member or loved one who requires artificial nutrition to stay alive. Some family members may want to continue the artificial nutrition. Other family members may not want to. Who gets to decide when caregivers disagree? Sometimes the cases go to court. One case in Wisconsin went to the Wisconsin Supreme Court.

Read this court case about a patient on artificial nutrition.

A 71-year-old woman was being cared for by her sister and another guardian who had been appointed by the court. The woman suffered from Alzheimer's dementia and was no longer able to care for herself. She could not get out of bed. Doctors said that she responded to voices and was alert sometimes. Sometimes her eyes were open. Artificial nutrition was given via a tube, and she continued breathing without any aid.

Seven years later, the woman's sister and guardian wanted to remove the artificial nutrition. They said that the woman would not want to live like this. They asked the state's Supreme Court to consider their case.

If you were a judge on the state's Supreme Court, what would you do? Write two or three reasons for your decision.

_____

_____

_____

_____

Would you consider an earlier case in which the court said that an incompetent person in a persistent vegetative state could be withdrawn from artificial nutrition? What makes that case similar or different?

_____

_____

_____

_____

Work with a small group. Discuss your decisions and reasons. Add up the decisions for and against. What did you decide? Present your decisions to the rest of the class.

_____

_____

_____

_____

# Part 3: The Food Groups

## Pre-Listening Activities

The Center for Nutrition Policy and Promotion is one part of the U.S. Department of Agriculture. One goal of the organization is to improve the nutrition and well-being of Americans by providing diet guidelines and conducting research about nutrition. It offers suggestions about which foods to eat and how much of each should be eaten in an effort to make Americans healthier and happier. Answer these questions with a partner.

1. Is there an organization that creates dietary guidelines in other countries? Do you think a government agency can guide its citizens on what to eat? Do you think you would follow the guidelines? Why or why not?

   _____

   _____

   _____

2. What food groups can you name? What items do you think fall into each group?

   _____

   _____

   _____

3. Describe your diet during a typical week. How do you think it compares to the U.S. government guidelines? Do you think you meet government recommendations?

   _____

   _____

   _____

## Strategy: Preparing before a Lecture

Instructors often tell you what will be discussed in the next class. Many times you can look at the course syllabus to see what topics will be covered. Previewing the topic before the lecture can improve your listening comprehension.

- ✓ Read the corresponding textbook material.
- ✓ Look at figures, illustrations, or other graphic materials.
- ✓ Do an online search for the title or keywords.
- ✓ Write questions you have about the topic.
- ✓ Plan a way to organize your notes.

### Preparing before a Lecture

Follow the instructions, and write a short answer to each question.

1. Perform an online keyword search for the lecture title: "Nutrition: The Food Groups." Summarize your findings.

   _____

   _____

   _____

2. Look at this illustration and the corresponding course materials on pages 65–66. Combined with the keyword search, what questions do you have about the topic?

From U.S. Department of Agriculture, www.mypyramid.gov/downloads/MiniPoster.pdf. Accessed on February 1, 2010.

_____

_____

_____

3. Read the corresponding text the instructor listed as required reading material. What other keyword searches would you do?

_____

_____

_____

(Question 4 is on page 66.)

# Reading

Read the article about oils from the U.S. Department of Agriculture before listening to the lecture.

INSIDE THE PYRAMID

What are *oils*?

Oils are fats that are liquid at room temperature, like the vegetable oils used in cooking. Oils come from many different plants and from fish. Some common oils are:

- canola oil
- corn oil
- cottonseed oil
- olive oil
- safflower oil
- soybean oil
- sunflower oil

Some oils are used mainly as flavorings, such as walnut oil and sesame oil. A number of foods are naturally high in oils, like:

- nuts
- olives
- some fish
- avocados

Foods that are mainly oil include mayonnaise, certain salad dressings, and soft (tub or squeeze) margarine with no *trans* fats. Check the Nutrition Facts label to find margarines with 0 grams of *trans* fat. Amounts of *trans* fat were required on labels as of 2006.

Most oils are high in monounsaturated or polyunsaturated fats, and low in saturated fats. Oils from plant sources (vegetable and nut oils) do not contain any cholesterol. In fact, no foods from plants sources contain cholesterol.

A few plant oils, however, including coconut oil and palm kernel oil, are high in saturated fats and for nutritional purposes should be considered to be solid fats.

Solid fats are fats that are solid at room temperature, like butter and shortening. Solid fats come from many animal foods and can be made from vegetable oils through a process called hydrogenation. Some common solid fats are:

- butter
- beef fat (tallow, suet)
- chicken fat
- pork fat (lard)
- stick margarine
- shortening

From U.S. Department of Agriculture, www.mypyramid.gov/pyramid/oils.html. Accessed on February 1, 2010.

4. What new questions do you have about the topic?

_____

_____

_____

Compare answers with a small group. What questions did you write? What other information do you think the instructor might include in the lecture?

## Note-Taking

### Strategy: Using a Chart to Organize Lists

An easy way to collect and remember information is to make lists. A good form to use is a chart. Sometimes you can prepare a chart in advance if you've performed a keyword search and looked at corresponding readings.

A chart you may create from your research on food groups might look like this:

| Groups | Examples |
|---|---|
| Grains | |
| Vegetables | |
| Fruits | |
| Milk | |
| Meat and Beans | |

A good strategy is to leave room for other sections of the chart so you can add to it as the instructor lectures. For example, you may have asked a question about the reading on oils. Where would you add room in the chart for oils? What other information might you want to include? A chart allows you to add columns and rows for additional notes.

## Adding Categories to a Note-Taking Chart

Listen to the first part of the lecture. What other note-taking categories would you add? Write them in the chart.

| Groups | Examples | |
|---|---|---|
| Grains | | |
| Vegetables | | |
| Fruits | | |
| Milk | | |
| Meat and Beans | | |
| | | |

**Vocabulary Power**

There are a number of terms and phrases in this lecture that you may encounter in other academic settings. Add at least five vocabulary items to your vocabulary notebook or log.

Match the words in bold from the lecture on the left with a definition on the right.

1. _____ There are many factors that are considered when determining the **quantity** needed.

a. suggestions

b. proof

2. _____ Most notably, they **reduce** the risk of heart disease and can help with weight management.

c. amount

d. necessary

3. _____ It may be an **ideal** way for women and men to get the vegetables they need; two and a half cups of vegetables for women, three for men.

e. perfect

f. better

4. _____ Consuming the daily **recommendations** of vegetables produces such health benefits as . . .

g. lower

h. match, look like

5. _____ The health benefits **mirror** those of vegetables.

6. _____ Because it's low in fat, grabbing a banana for a snack is **superior** to reaching for that chocolate bar.

7. _____ Some **evidence** suggests that omega-3 fatty acids in fish can reduce the risk of mortality from cardiovascular disease.

8. _____ Why does the USDA bother to put them on the pyramid? First, they're a great source of Vitamin E. Second, oils contain **essential** fatty acids.

## Listening 3: Food Groups

### Listening to a Lecture

The listening passage is a lecture from a health class. The instructor is discussing the dietary guidelines offered by the U.S. Department of Agriculture and the food guide pyramid that illustrates the food groups. Use the chart on page 68 to write notes as you listen to the lecture on the five food groups.

### Checking Your Understanding: Main Ideas

Review your note-taking chart. Listen again to the lecture if necessary, and then put a check mark (✓) next to the statements that best reflect the main ideas.

_____ Oils should be considered a sixth food group.

_____ Each food group has its own recommended quantities, health benefits, and nutrients.

_____ All the food groups have some benefits and some implications.

_____ Grains are ever-important, but items in the meat and beans group are not as important.

_____ Each food group has many examples of items that can be included in a healthy diet.

### Checking Your Understanding: Details

Use your note-taking chart, and put a check mark (✓) next to the best answers. Some questions have more than one answer.

1. Daily allowances were given for people up to what age?

   a. _____ 13

   b. _____ 19

   c. _____ 30

   d. _____ 90

2. Which food groups are good nutritional sources of B vitamins?

a. _____ grains

b. _____ vegetables

c. _____ fruits

d. _____ meat and beans

3. Which food groups reduce a person's risk of strokes?

a. _____ grains

b. _____ vegetables

c. _____ fruits

d. _____ meat and beans

4. How many servings from the milk group does the average man or woman need per day?

a. _____ 2 cups

b. _____ 3 cups

c. _____ 6 cups

d. _____ 7 cups

5. Why are beans a vegetable, also a part of the meat and beans group?

a. _____ because they contain acids that reduce mortality from cardiovascular disease

b. _____ because they contain protein like most meats

c. _____ because it is healthier to reach the daily allowance with beans rather than meat

d. _____ because they contain healthy oils

6. What important nutrient do oils contain?

a. _____ B

b. _____ C

c. _____ D

d. _____ E

**Evaluating Your Notes**

Look back at your note-taking chart on page 68. Answer these questions.

1. Were there any categories you needed but didn't have on your chart?

   _____

   _____

   _____

2. Were there any categories you had on the chart but didn't need?

   _____

   _____

   _____

3. Were any of your questions answered during the lecture?

   _____

   _____

   _____

4. What would you change about your chart? Compare your new chart with a partner's.

   _____

   _____

   _____

   _____

   _____

## Discussion

In the video, the students express agreement and disagreement and discussed pros and cons about artificial nutrition. Discussing many options and the positive and negative things about each is an important part of academic group work.

Imagine you are a team of nutritionists working for a university health center. You have three patients (described on page 74) who want or need to lose weight but need help beyond what a normal diet can provide. Study the list of options and discuss the pros and cons of each patient using these weight-loss techniques. You can add other ideas to the list. Then, prepare to present your recommendations on the patient you think you can help the most.

### WEIGHT-LOSS TECHNIQUES

Brush your teeth immediately after eating

Don't eat after 7 PM

Drink a lot of water

Eat at home or pack your lunch

Eat five small meals a day

Eat slowly

Eat what you want, but in smaller portions

Indulge in a dessert only one time a week

Join a diet group

Sleep more

Skip meals

Take the steps instead of the elevator

Use smaller plates for your meals

Walk up and down steps for 15 minutes

**PATIENT 1**

Melia is a freshman at the university. Since starting classes, she has gained 15 pounds and many of her clothes don't fit anymore. She's taking five classes, and two of those have additional study sessions. Her classes start at 8 AM and run through 7 PM. She grabs dinner, but then she goes to the library until midnight every night. She skips breakfast, eats at the dormitory cafeteria for lunch and dinner, and buys snacks from the vending machine while she is at the library.

**PATIENT 2**

Joe is a graduate student at the university. Ever since he was young, he has been at least 25 pounds overweight. Obesity runs in his family. He stays on diets, but he still doesn't seem to lose weight. He is worried that his weight will lead to diabetes or other medical conditions. He says he needs some new ideas because he is often sitting at his desk working on his thesis.

**PATIENT 3**

Dr. Leebun is a professor in the Division of Humanities. She was recently promoted to be the chairperson of her department. This position requires more paperwork and more time. She had to stop going to the gym three times a week. She feels she is eating more and more food since she has to spend so much time working at her desk instead of teaching. She is trying to stay on a diet, but she is having trouble.

Our patient: _____

Our ideas:

_____

_____

Pros and cons:

_____

_____

Our final recommendations:

_____

_____

**Rapid Vocabulary Review**

From the three answers on the right, circle the one that best explains, is an example of, or combines with the vocabulary item on the left as it is used in this unit.

| Vocabulary | Answers | | |
|---|---|---|---|
| Synonyms | | | |
| 1. withdraw | provide | manage | remove |
| 2. sustain | apply | frown | keep |
| 3. glance | state strongly | destroy | look at quickly |
| 4. a facet | a fact | an aspect | a source |
| 5. fatigue | tiredness | hunger | certainty |
| 6. essential | lazy | risky | necessary |
| 7. artificial | very beautiful | not natural | only one person |
| 8. means (of) | facts | methods | troubles |
| 9. up to 10 | 7, 8, 9 | 10, 11, 12 | 10, 20, 30 |
| 10. administer | give | take | eat |
| 11. reduce | destroy | decrease | develop |
| 12. prevent | predict | encourage | stop |
| Combinations and Associations | | | |
| 13. to get rid ___ | of | to | with |
| 14. are ___ of | aware | bothered | essential |
| 15. skip ___ | a computer | a newspaper | a meal |
| 16. a ___ category | cloudy | gold | broad |
| 17. in spite ___ | with | to | of |
| 18. is superior ___ | from | to | into |
| 19. convey a ___ | message | person | song |
| 20. to begin ___ | about | to | with |

## ⇨✂⇦ Synthesizing: Projects and Presentations

| Short In-Class Speaking Assignments | Longer Outside Assignments |
|---|---|
| Impromptu Speech | My Own Pyramid |
| Your teacher will name one of the five food groups. State your favorite food from that group and talk for one minute about why you like it and any pros or cons to making your favorite a regular part of your diet. | Record everything you eat or drink for three days in a note-taking chart that contains the five food groups. Study the recommended daily amounts on the pyramid. Add a third column to your chart detailing what you would like to change about your diet and how you plan to do so. |
| The Ideal Cafeteria | The Perfect Plan |
| Work with a small group to open a new cafeteria at your school . . . one that serves only healthy food choices. Decide on one specialty meal that you would serve for each of the main meals: breakfast, lunch, and dinner. Present your menu to the class. | Use the U.S. Department of Agriculture website to create an ideal diet for a 20-year-old male who is 5 feet and 11 inches tall and weighs 180 pounds. Once you've determined his daily amounts, decide how he should eat those, including which foods and at which meals. Think about how he should prepare those. Then present your plan to the class. |

**Vocabulary Log**

To increase your vocabulary knowledge, write a definition or translation for each vocabulary item. Then write an original phrase, sentence, or note that will help you remember the vocabulary item.

| Vocabulary Item | Definition or Translation | Your Original Phrase, Sentence, or Note |
|---|---|---|
| 1. portion | a part, a share | restaurant serves large portions |
| 2. vital | | |
| 3. a sliver | | |
| 4. withhold | | |
| 5. per se | | |
| 6. substantial | | |
| 7. a rank | | |
| 8. susceptible | | |
| 9. appropriate | | |
| 10. consume | | |
| 11. such as | | |
| 12. subsequent | | |
| 13. quantity | | |
| 14. evidence | | |

| Vocabulary Item | Definition or Translation | Your Original Phrase, Sentence, or Note |
|---|---|---|
| 15. claim (n.) | | |
| 16. nutrition | | |
| 17. figure out | | |
| 18. overall | | |
| 19. sacrifice | | |
| 20. as of (2006) | | |
| 21. a stroke | | |
| 22. range | | |
| 23. mirror (v.) | | |
| 24. corresponding | | |
| 25. nevertheless | | |

# 3 Business:
## The World of Entrepreneurship

A business department at a university offers many courses to prepare people for finance careers in the business world. Course topics include accounting, marketing, human resources, and management. Entrepreneurship is one aspect of business in which a person, or team, starts a new company or business rather than work for a more established organization. This unit explores the world of entrepreneurship— is it rewarding . . . or risky?

# Part 1: Characteristics of an Entrepreneur

## Pre-Listening Activities

Entrepreneurs create their own company rather than work for an existing company. There are benefits to having your own company, but there are also challenges and risks. Do entrepreneurs have certain personality and business characteristics that not everyone shares? Answer these questions with a partner.

1. Bill Gates, Walt Disney, and Ray Kroc (of McDonald's fame) are famous entrepreneurs. List other entrepreneurs you are familiar with and their companies that grew from an idea into a large company.

   _____

   _____

   _____

2. What are some advantages and disadvantages to starting a business?

   Ad: Have chances to make a lot of money and can have an unusual experience.

   Disad: Too risky and it will take a long time and hardly have a rest.

3. Do you think you would like to be an entrepreneur? Why or why not?

   _____

   _____

   _____

## Strategy: Getting the Gist (General Idea)

It is important to remember that you don't need to understand every word in order to understand the gist—the main idea. There are several things you can try to do in order to get the gist of the conversation, discussion, or lecture.

✓ Focus on the words that you are familiar with.

✓ Don't panic when you don't understand a word. Try to guess the meaning from the context.

✓ Listen for general information, not details.

✓ Ask for clarification (see Unit 1, page 6).

### Answering Questions about the Gist

Read the passage. Guess what the missing words are using the context. Then answer the questions on page 82.

Since its _____ on July 30, 1953, the U.S. Small Business Administration has _____ millions of loans, loan guarantees, _____, counseling _____, and other forms of assistance to small _____.

The SBA was officially _____ in 1953, but its philosophy and _____ began _____ _____ years earlier in a number of _____ agencies, largely as a response _____ of the _____ _____ and World War II.

The Reconstruction Finance Corporation (RFC), created by President Hoover in 1932 to _____ the financial crisis of the Great Depression, was SBA's grandparent. The RFC was _____ a federal _____ program for all businesses hurt by the Depression, large and small. It was _____ as the personal project of Hoover's successor, President Franklin D. Roosevelt, and was _____ by some of Roosevelt's most capable and dedicated workers.

Adapted from www.sba.gov/aboutsba/history/index.html. Accessed February 1, 2010.

1. When did the Small Business Administration start?

_____ *1953* _____

2. What is one of its primary functions?

_____ *RFC* _____

3. Why was the SBA started?

_____

4. Why was the RFC formed?

_____ *financial systems* _____

---

**Checking Your Guesses**

Read the complete version of the passage online, or get the answers from your instructor. Check your guesses. Then answer the questions.

1. How many blanks did you fill in? ____ *5 / 5*

2. How many did you fill in correctly? ____ *3*

3. Were some of your guesses close to the correct meaning? *Yes  No*

4. Did having blanks or not having the exact word prevent you from getting at least part of the gist? ____ *Yes*

5. Do you think you can get the gist of a conversation or lecture without knowing every word? Be prepared to discuss your ideas with a small group.

_____

_____

_____

# Listening 1: Getting the Main Idea

## Listening for Information

The listening passage is a conversation between a student and the teacher assistant for his business class. They are discussing entrepreneurs and some personality traits that many entrepreneurs seem to share. As you listen to the conversation, circle the best answer.

1. How many traits do all entrepreneurs share?

   a. 0

   b. 1

   c. 3

   d. 4

2. According to the passage, which of these words can be used to describe entrepreneurs? <u>Note</u>: This word was not used in the passage, but the gist was evident.

   a. worried

   b. strong

   c. busy

   d. happy

3. Based on the information in the conversation, which statement is true?

   a. All entrepreneurs share the same traits that propel them to success.

   b. Most entrepreneurs have been successful in fields involving the Internet, publishing, and fast food.

   c. The traits are shared by people in a variety of careers.

   d. Certain traits are required to be successful in any career.

4. What will the study session on Thursday will NOT cover?

   a. time management

   b. traits shared with other professions

   c. industriousness and perseverance

   d. leadership skills

**Speaking**

### Asking Questions

It is easy to get lost in a conversation, especially when the vocabulary is unfamiliar. You should not allow the speaker to continue talking when you really do not know what the speaker is saying. As soon as you are unsure of the gist, stop the conversation by asking a clarification question. Review the information on page 6 in Unit 1. It is helpful to be able to ask a direct question about the thing you are not sure of. Ask what it is or ask for an example. Some phrases that you can use are given.

ASKING FOR . . .

| . . . an Example |
| --- |
| *Like what?* |
| *Could you give me an example?* |
| *Such as?* |
| *What would that be similar to?* |

| . . . a Definition |
| --- |
| *So what does X mean?* |
| *What exactly does X mean?* |
| *What is X?* |
| *How would you define X?* |

If you are the speaker and someone asks you for information, you will have to give an example or definition. Some common phrases that you can use to start your responses are shown.

GIVING . . .

| . . . an Example |
| --- |
| *For example, . . .* |
| *To illustrate, . . .* |
| *Such as . . .* |
| *It's like . . .* |

| . . . a Definition |
| --- |
| *It means. . .* |
| *The definition I know is . . .* |
| *It is . . .* |
| *Another word for it is . . .* |

## Role-Playing

Work with a classmate to role play possible conversations about famous entrepreneurs. Choose names and traits from the boxes to use in your dialogues. Then read your dialogue for the class.

| ENTREPRENEURS | |
| --- | --- |
| Richard Branson (music) | Milton Hershey (candy) |
| Debbi Fields (cookies) | Ray Kroc (fast food) |
| Henry Ford (automobiles) | Estee Lauder (makeup) |
| Bill Gates (computers) | Sam Walton (retail) |
| Joyce Hall (greeting cards) | Oprah Winfrey (entertainment) |

| TRAITS | | |
| --- | --- | --- |
| aggressive | industrious | nice |
| dedicated | intelligent | patient |
| difficult | loyal | quiet |
| diligent | mean | responsible |
| friendly | motivated | selfish |
| funny | nervous | stubborn |

Person A begins by asking Person B if he or she has heard of a certain entrepreneur.

Person B responds affirmatively or negatively.

Person A describes the entrepreneur.

Person B asks for a definition of the trait.

Person A gives a definition.

Person B asks for an example of another entrepreneur.

Person A gives another example.

Person A: 

_____

Person B: 

_____

Person A: 

_____

Person B:

_____

Person A:

_____

Person B:

_____

Person A:

_____

Change roles.

Person A:

_____

Person B:

_____

Person A:

_____

Person B:

_____

Person A:

_____

Person B:

_____

Person A:

_____

## Making an Impromptu Speech

Give a two-minute speech on an entrepreneur you most identify with and the personality traits that you believe you share with that person.

## Part 2: Developing a Company

### Pre-Listening Activities

As you learned in Part 1, many entrepreneurs share certain qualities. Imagine for a moment that you have the ideal personality and have an idea for a new business. You need unlimited funds from a wealthy investor with which to start the new business. Answer these questions with a partner.

1. What kind of business would you want to start? Why?

   _____

   _____

   _____

2. What convincing arguments could you give the wealthy investor about why he or she should support your business?

   _____

   _____

   _____

3. What are some arguments the wealthy investor might pose?

   _____

   _____

   _____

## Strategy: Listening for and Using Persuasion

In English, certain words are stressed more than others. By identifying which words are being stressed, you can often understand the speaker's point of view. Emphasizing words also helps convey emotion. This can be helpful if you need to persuade someone of your point of view during an academic discussion. There are several strategies you should listen for or use during a discussion when decisions need to be made.

✓ Stress content words: nouns, verbs, adjectives, and adverbs.

My restaurant will have good pizza and drivers will come to campus.

✓ Use stronger, longer, or less frequent, content words.

My amazing restaurant will serve the best pizza, and the drivers will conveniently deliver to campus.

✓ Add emotion and exclamation.

My amazing restaurant will serve the best pizza. Pizza that I wished had been available when I was a student. The drivers will conveniently deliver to campus—any time day or night!

*Pronunciation Note*: You can stress a word one of three ways or by using a combination of more than one.

- Increase your volume (say it louder than normal)
- Use a strong vowel sound (say it longer than normal)
- Raise your pitch (say it higher than normal)

### Practicing Persuasion

Complete the sentences. Insert or replace content words and add emotion and exclamation. Say them to a partner, expressing yourself persuasively. Then change roles.

1. I am a ___business___ major because I like the subject.

2. My favorite place to eat on campus is ___Panda___ because it has good food.

3. On weekends, I like to ___play games___ because it is fun.

4. If I could open a business, I would open a ___restaurant___ uniform company because
   ___I can provide very beautiful clothes for costumers___.

5. My favorite movie is ___Transformer___; it's a good movie.

6. You should travel to ___Xiaoshan___. It's the best place I've been.

7. If I had a million dollars, I would ___buy a new car and a new house___

## Speaking

### Persuading and Countering

In conversations and group discussions, you will sometimes have to agree on one idea or topic for a group project. You will want to persuade people to hear your ideas or reasons. Some phrases that you can use to begin your persuasive statements are given. Your choice of phrase and your tone of voice are important. Consider who you are talking with and what you are talking about when choosing the best words and tone to use.

PERSUADING

| |
|---|
| *You have to remember that . . .* |
| *Wouldn't you agree that . . .* |
| *Don't you think that . . .* |
| *Everyone recognizes that . . .* |
| *You must see my point that . . .* |
| *Don't forget to consider that . . .* |

Sometimes you will need to counter someone else's persuasive comments. You should have a good reason for your counter. Some phrases that you can use before delivering your counterargument are listed.

COUNTERING

| |
|---|
| *Well . . .* |
| *But . . .* |
| *I'll grant you that, however. . .* |
| *Still, I think. . .* |
| *Nevertheless. . .* |
| *Even though that may be true, . . .* |
| *The issue remains. . .* |

After a counter, you can either counter again, or you can concede. If you concede, it means that you have been persuaded to some degree. Some good phrases to use to offer concession are shown.

CONCEDING

| |
|---|
| *I see what you mean.* |
| *I do agree with that point.* |
| *I can go along with that idea.* |
| *That makes sense.* |
| *Sure.* |
| *Okay.* |

## Role-Playing

Work with a classmate to role play possible conversations for these situations. Use the phrases in the boxes or others that you can think of to write dialogues. Then exchange roles. Read your dialogues to the class.

SITUATIONS

1. You want to be an entrepreneur. You're going to quit college and start a business.

2. You're studying what your parents want you to, but you really want to be a movie star. You're going to tell your parents that you're leaving school and going to Hollywood to pursue your dreams of acting.

3. You think the tuition for classes has skyrocketed. You're going to make an appointment with the president of the student body to demand something be done.

4. You have gained 15 pounds since starting school. You're going to consume only liquids in an effort to lose weight.

Person A begins by stating his or her intention.

Person B will try to persuade Person A to rethink his or her intention.

Person A will counter.

Person B will counter or concede.

Person A will counter or concede.

Person A:

_____

Person B:

_____

Person A:

_____

Person B:

_____


Can you extend the conversions by continuing to counter rather than conceding?
Don't concede until you can't think of any more strong arguments.

_____

_____

_____

_____

_____

# Listening 2: Persuading Team Members

**Listening in Groups**

Listen to the students discuss ideas for a new business that they have to start for their business class. Discuss the questions in a small group.

**Focus on Language**

1. What persuading phrases are used? What other persuasion strategies are used (see page 88)? <u>Note</u>: Don't worry about writing exact words.

    We never ___ complete.
    still ___ we could ___ I think we need

2. What phrases are used to counter? <u>Note</u>: Don't worry about writing exact words.

    but, still
    that's an idea but, Maybe

3. What phrases are used to express concession? <u>Note</u>: Don't worry about writing exact words.

*Maybe*

_____

_____

4. Write any phrases or idioms that you are not familiar with. Discuss what they mean and in what type of interactions they are appropriate.

_____

_____

**Focus on Tone**

1. Does each speaker use a tone of voice that is appropriate for the word choice and situation? Why or why not?

_____

_____

2. Which speaker uses the most persuasive tone? Does it match his or her words?

_____

_____

3. If you could advise one of the students about tone, who would you advise to change? What advice would you offer?

_____

_____

## Focus on Nonverbal Communication

1. What nonverbal cues are used when persuading?

   _____

   _____

2. What nonverbal cues are used when countering?

   _Crossed arms_        _shark hands_ _____

   _____

3. What nonverbal cues are used when conceding?

   _____

   _____

4. Which student do you think has the most expressive facial expressions? Does this positively or negatively affect the interaction?

   _____

   _____

## Summary

1. How strongly do you think the speakers feel about their ideas? What evidence is there to support your opinion?

   _confident_ _____

   _____

2. Whose business idea do you like the best? What is it about that argument that persuaded you?

   _____

   _____

3. Is there anyone that you wouldn't want to work with to open a new business? Why?

   _____

   _____

## Discussion

The students in the video discuss new business ideas for a restaurant, bookstore, article of clothing, a school supply. Work with a group to develop one of those four ideas. You can continue to develop one of their ideas or create a new twist on one of their ideas. Take notes about your business, and be prepared to present your business to the class.

Product or Idea: _____

Audience: _____

Who is our competition?

_____

_____

_____

What is special about our product or idea?

_____

_____

_____

What are our goals?

_____

_____

_____

How will we achieve our goals? What are our strategies to get customers?

_____

_____

_____

# You Be the Judge

Should everyone be free to start a new business?

Read this court case about a taxi entrepreneur.

> In one American city, an official taxi organization wanted no new competition.
> However, one aspiring taxi entrepreneur wanted to enter the market. He had tried
> for several years to provide taxi service in the city only to be refused entry into the
> market. Existing taxi companies filed a lawsuit citing an older law that it excluded
> entrepreneurs from entering the market for ten years. The taxi driver's lawyer
> claimed that not only did this keep his client from choosing the career of his
> choice, but it also was hurting the people of the city because it deprived them
> of another choice in taxis.

If you were the judge, what would you do? Would you stand by the existing law
that protects the taxi organization or would you vote in favor of the entrepreneur? Write two or three reasons for your decision.

I will let several taxi company exist.
Because it's good for competiting, and can control the price of
taxi. it's good for citizen.

Work with a small group. Discuss your decisions and your reasons. Come to a
group consensus. What did you decide? Present your decisions to the rest of the
class.

# Part 3: Analyzing a New Business

## Pre-Listening Activities

Entrepreneurs and business people have to analyze their product, idea, or business to determine its strengths and weaknesses and how successful it will be against its competition. A good analysis will also think about external factors that could help or hurt the company.

Think about a new restaurant that sells more expensive, but healthier food options. Answer these questions with a partner.

1. What strengths might this new kind of restaurant have?

   environment , serves food quality

2. What challenges might the restaurant face?

   No consumer, location, servies manage
   high cost

3. What are some external factors that might affect how successful a restaurant will be regardless of what food it serves?

   epidemic disease, economic crisis

## Strategy: Listening for and Using Boundary Signal Words

Instructors often give examples and details about the main ideas. Think of a boundary line between cities or countries. That line indicates a change between two things. The instructor uses signal words to indicate a "boundary" between topics, examples, or details.

### Ordinal Numbers

*first, second, third*

> The first thing to consider is. . .
>
> Second, I will discuss . . .

### Time Words

*before, after, during, earlier, later, while*

> Before moving on, let me give you an example of. . .
>
> After I tell you what SWOT stands for, I will define each area.
>
> During the lecture, I will define each word and give examples.

### Process Words

*then, next, now*

> Now, let me turn your attention to a new business venture.

## Listening and Using Boundary Signal Words

Describe these processes using words from the box on page 98 or other signals that you can think of. Be prepared to describe your process to the class.

1. How I Make My Favorite Food

   _____

   _____

   _____

   _____

   _____

2. How I Prepare to Study

   _____

   _____

   _____

   _____

   _____

3. My Typical Monday

   _____

   _____

   _____

   _____

   _____

## Note-Taking

### Strategy: Taking Notes on Visual Aids

Many instructors use a chalk or white board or electronic slides during their lectures. Often, the information on the board or slide contains the headings or main points and some general information. The lecture will contain more details, but you can use the headings and general information as a guide to help you figure out what to include in your notes.

# Reading

## Reading about the Small Business Administration

It's easy to see the main headings and subheadings in a textbook or other printed source. Read this article about the Small Business Administration and highlight the main headings. Highlight the subheadings in another color. Last, highlight the details in a third color.

## The U.S. Small Business Administration (SBA):

With a portfolio of business loans, loan guarantees, and venture capital instruments worth nearly $85 billion—including a disaster loan portfolio of more than $10 billion—the SBA is the nation's largest single financial backer of small businesses.

### What is the SBA?

A small, independent federal agency of the United States government.

Mandate: Aid, counsel, assist and protect the interests of small business concerns, preserve free competitive enterprise, maintain and strengthen the overall economy of the nation, and assist in the economic recovery of communities after disasters.

The Fiscal Year 2008 budget—approximately $570 million. The SBA's budget is appropriated annually through Congress.

This represents 2.23/100 of 1% of the total federal budget, yet the SBA is one of the 5 largest federal credit agencies.

### History:

Created by the Small Business Act in 1953.

Predecessor Institutions: The Smaller War Plants Corporation, the Reconstruction Finance Corporation, Office of Small Business, and the Small Defense Plants Administration.

Service Delivery Structure: Through SBA's 90 regional and district and branch offices

Also through SBA's financial participants and resource partners.

## U.S. Small Businesses:

- Represent more than 99.7 percent of all employers.
- Generate 60 to 80 percent of net new jobs annually.
- Employ more than half of all private sector workers.
- Pay more than 45 percent of the total U.S. private payroll.
- Provide over 50 percent of non-farm private gross domestic product (GDP).

Adapted from Office of Entrepreneurial Development, "An Introduction to the U.S. Small Business Administration," page 1. Accessed February 1, 2010 at www.sba.gov/idc/groups/public/documents/sba_homepage/serv_abt_overview_english.pdf.

### Identifying Headings in Lectures

Work with a partner, and read the text about the Small Business Administration again. Answer these questions.

1. If you had to present information to your classmates, how many slides would you have? What information would you use as headings on slides?

   *4.*

   *Influence of SBA.*

2. Write an introduction to your presentation stating what information you will include about the Small Business Administration and in what order. Use sequence signal words between each heading for which you would have a slide.

**Vocabulary Power**

There are a number of terms and phrases in this lecture that you may encounter in other academic settings. Add at least five vocabulary items to your vocabulary notebook or log.

Match the words in bold from the lecture on the left with a definition on the right.

1. ___ Today we're going to talk about a tool that new and established businesses alike use to analyze a product, idea, or business **venture**: a SWOT analysis.

a. formed by opinion rather than fact

b. achieving something quickly

2. ___ . . . I'll show you a **template** of a SWOT analysis . . .

c. to believe to be true

3. ___ . . . **attributes** that will enhance or serve as a benefit—meaning they will help the company achieve success.

d. an undertaking that involves chance or risk

4. ___ Rather than benefitting the company, though, these are attributes that will harm or hurt the company's performance and could potentially **render** the company a failure.

e. characteristics or qualities

5. ___ Opportunities can be defined as conditions or factors that are helpful to **vaulting** your company to success but that come from outside the company.

f. a pattern or form used to collect standard information

6. ___ While we're on the topic, let's talk about another opportunity: **mergers** or alliances with other companies—joint agreements if you will.

g. companies being absorbed or taken over by another

7. ___ . . . some other **perceived** threats are: taxes that may be added onto your product, political issues, a weak economy, or even bad weather.

h. to cause to become

8. ___ Although SWOT analyses are **subjective**, they are comprised of logically organized information from which decisions can be made.

# Listening 3: Analyzing a New Business

## Listening to a Lecture

The listening passage is a lecture from a business class. The instructor is discussing a tool some businesses use when trying to develop a new product or that entrepreneurs use to analyze a new company. Use the headings on the slides to organize your notes as you listen to the lecture on SWOT analyses. Write your notes next to the slide that would be shown when the instructor is giving the details.

Slide 1

<table>
<tr><td>

A SWOT Analysis

Definitions, Examples, Template

</td><td>

4 things

discussion about Bussiness

</td></tr>
</table>

Slide 2

<table>
<tr><td>

Strengths—Definition

</td><td>

Company for conducts

</td></tr>
</table>

Slide 3

| Strengths—Examples |
| business to sucess |

*bussiness to sucess*

*Marketing*
*cheap price*
*material*

Slide 4

| Weaknesses—Definition |

*Internal*
*can't be improved*
*potential.*

Slide 5

| Weaknesses—Examples |

*no bf ad.*

Slide 6

| Opportunities—Definition |
| --- |
| |

conditions the or factors
helpful to success

Slide 7

| Opportunities—Examples |
| --- |
| |

competitive
Customers.

Slide 8

| Threats—Definition |
| --- |
| |

a good way to
internal

Slide 9

> Threats—Examples

small
I who open a bussines, detroy
your bussness
Tax, porcdunct economy tisue .

Slide 10

> SWOT Template

faur squares , oppor tunroy

## Checking Your Understanding: Main Ideas

Review your notes. Listen again to the lecture if necessary, and then put a check mark (✓) next to the statements that best reflect the main ideas.

_____ A SWOT analysis is used to analyze the potential of a new product or business.

✓ _____ Strengths and weaknesses are internal factors that a businessperson can control.

_____ There are many examples of the four areas in a SWOT analysis.

_____ The four parts of a SWOT analysis are subjective and organized.

✓ _____ An organic food restaurant is a good example to use when developing a SWOT analysis.

## Checking Your Understanding: Details

Use your notes, and put a check mark (✓) next to the best answers. Some questions have more than one answer.

1. Which of the four parts of a SWOT analysis consider the benefits to the company?

   a. _____ strengths
   b. _____ weaknesses
   c. _____ opportunities
   d. _____ threats

2. Marketing expertise is given as an example of which part(s) of the SWOT analysis?

   a. _____ strengths
   b. _____ weaknesses
   c. _____ opportunities
   d. _____ threats

3. Which are examples of external factors?

   a. _____ location

   b. _____ price

   c. _____ brand name

   d. _✓_ mergers

   e. _✓_ economy

4. What does the instructor imply is the biggest threat?

   a. a bad economy

   b. a new competitor

   c. no advertising budget

   d. bad weather

5. Which design best illustrates what a SWOT template may look like?

| Strengths | Weaknesses |
|---|---|
| Threats | Opportunities |

| Strengths | Opportunities |
|---|---|
| Weaknesses | Threats |

| Strengths | Threats |
|---|---|
| Weaknesses | Opportunities |

| Strengths | Weaknesses |
|---|---|
| Opportunities | Threats |

## Creating a SWOT Analysis

Work with your entrepreneurial team from Part 2. Create a SWOT analysis for the business you created. Present your analysis to the class.

|  |  |
|  |  |
|  |  |

## Debate

Divide the class into two teams. One team will discuss the pros to working for a large, established company (and the cons to being an entrepreneur). The other team will discuss the pros to entrepreneurship (and the cons to working for a large, established company).

Topic: Entrepreneurship

Pro or Con: _____

Choose one team member to give an introductory statement and one to give a closing statement. Divide the arguments evenly among the remaining team members. You will need to be prepared to disagree, and counter at least one point from the other team. Each statement, argument, and counterargument lasts for two minutes.

Follow this debate format:

Pro team member gives an introductory statement on the topic to present/preview pro opinion

Con team gives an introductory statement on the topic to present/preview con opinion

Con team member delivers first argument

Pro team member rebuts with counterargument

Pro team member delivers next argument

Con team member rebuts with counterargument

Team members will continue exchanging arguments and rebuttals until all team members have delivered their arguments and counterarguments.

Open discussion (10 minutes)

Pro team member gives a closing statement/summary on pro team's argument

Con team member gives a closing statement/summary on con team's argument

Team member giving introductory statement _____

Team member giving closing statement _____

Other arguments: _____

_____

_____

_____

_____

_____

## Preparing Individually

Think about the selected topic and then write two reasons that support your business type and two that are against your business type. You need to think about both sides so that you can argue effectively against the other team.

Pro 1:

_____

_____

_____

Pro 2:

_____

_____

_____

Con 1:

_____

_____

_____

Con 2:

_____

_____

_____

## Preparing as a Group

Now work with your team. Take turns discussing your pros and cons. Your group should select the strongest pros and cons to use during the debate. Select arguments that you think will be difficult for the other team to disagree with. Also think about responses you can use to counter the other team's arguments.

Arguments:

_____

_____

_____

_____

_____

_____

_____

Counterarguments:

_____

_____

_____

_____

_____

_____

_____

_____

**Rapid Vocabulary Review**

From the three answers on the right, circle the one that best explains, is an example of, or combines with the vocabulary item on the left as it is used in this unit.

| Vocabulary | Answers | | |
|---|---|---|---|
| Synonyms | | | |
| 1. harm | increase | complain | hurt |
| 2. risky | dangers | injuries | evils |
| 3. mean | not impressive | not nice | not selfish |
| 4. stubborn | no change possible | no template possible | no threat possible |
| 5. go along with an idea | want to improve an idea | agree with an idea | perceive an idea |
| 6. traits | characteristics | ventures | innovations |
| 7. a merger | an alliance | an obstacle | an economy |
| 8. a twist on something | a variation | an impression | a step back |
| 9. generate | commit | destroy | produce |
| 10. innovative | creative | productive | useful |
| 11. propose | do | try | suggest |
| 12. compile | persevere | collect | customize |
| Combinations and Associations | | | |
| 13. ___ you of | counter | achieve | deprive |
| 14. ___ a lawsuit | file | realize | pose |
| 15. drop ___ | after | by | on |
| 16. if ___ will | I | you | they |
| 17. a wealthy ___ | individual | automobile | career |
| 18. count me ___ | at | by | in |
| 19. go ___ | above | under | over |
| 20. ___ a conclusion | draw | keep | put |

## ⇨✕⊐ Synthesizing: Projects and Presentations

| Short In-Class Speaking Assignments | Longer Outside Assignments |
|---|---|
| My Personality Fits My Career Choice Because. . . | Guess the Entrepreneur |
| How does your personality make you a good fit for the career you'd like to pursue? Name what you think is a special personality trait and describe how it will help you be successful at the career you've chosen to pursue. Give a one-minute speech. | Do a little research and gather facts about a well-known entrepreneur. Bring 10 facts about your entrepreneur to class. Your classmates will have the chance to ask yes/no questions about your entrepreneur. See how many questions it takes before they figure out who you've chosen. Prepare a short biography of the entrepreneur you selected. |
| Strengths and Weaknesses | Convincing an Investor |
| What are your opportunities and threats? How will you take advantage of your opportunities to be successful academically, professionally, or both? Are there any external threats that may prevent you from being successful? How will you overcome them? Write a few notes and then share them with small group. | Write a marketing plan for a business you'd like to start. Include details about your product, who it is for, and what sets you apart from the competition. Prepare to talk about your strengths and counter your weaknesses. Present your plan a team of wealthy investors (your classmates) in an attempt to persuade them to supply funding for your venture. Be prepared to counter their arguments. Consider creating PowerPoint slides with headings so everyone can take notes on your main points. |

## Vocabulary Log

To increase your vocabulary knowledge, write a definition or translation for each vocabulary item. Then write an original phrase, sentence, or note that will help you remember the vocabulary item.

| Vocabulary Item | Definition or Translation | Your Original Phrase, Sentence, or Note |
|---|---|---|
| 1. rewarding | giving you satisfaction | a _____ experience |
| 2. perceive | | |
| 3. as long as | | |
| 4. pursue | | |
| 5. vain | | |
| 6. risky | | |
| 7. alliance | | |
| 8. potentially | | |
| 9. skyrocket | | |
| 10. I'll grant you that. | | |
| 11. convincing (adj.) | | |
| 12. threat | | |
| 13. loyal | | |
| 14. enterprise | | |

| Vocabulary Item | Definition or Translation | Your Original Phrase, Sentence, or Note |
|---|---|---|
| 15. subjective | | |
| 16. render | | |
| 17. key (n.) | | |
| 18. attribute | | |
| 19. external | | |
| 20. robust | | |
| 21. employ | | |
| 22. imply | | |
| 23. selfish | | |
| 24. aspiring (adj.) | | |
| 25. involve | | |

# 4 Mathematics: Math for Life

Mathematics is the study of numbers, space, patterns, and shapes and the relationships among them. Common courses include algebra, geometry, calculus, and trigonometry. Most people are required to take some math classes regardless of what hobbies they have or what industry they want to pursue. This unit focuses on how math plays a role in everyday life and in a variety of careers as well as part of its early beginnings in history.

# Part 1: Math in Everyday Life

## Pre-Listening Activities

Even though math isn't a favorite subject for everyone, it is something that plays a role in many facets of everyday life. Math is used for managing necessary household or educational tasks as well as participating in hobbies, sports, or other pastimes outside an educational or professional setting. Answer these questions with a partner.

1. What are some daily, weekly, or monthly tasks you have to do that require you to use math? What kind of math is involved?

   _____

   _____

   _____

2. What kind of leisure activities do you participate in that require the use of some math skills? What kind of math is involved?

   _____

   _____

   _____

3. Which of these activities have you participated in? Is the math associated with these activities easy or difficult? Do you know what kind of math is required for each?

   * calculated how much farther you had to drive while on vacation
   * determined how much of your paycheck goes to taxes
   * balanced your checkbook
   * converted money into another foreign currency
   * determined the price of something that was a certain percentage off
   * tipped a server at a restaurant
   * figured out how many pieces of tile you need to cover a floor
   * chipped in your share of a pizza

   _____

   _____

   _____

## Strategy: Listening for and Using Addition Signal Words and Phrases

Addition signal words and phrases let you know that there is more information to follow. These words and phrases help connect examples, reasons, and details together and help deliver strong arguments.

| | |
|---|---|
| also | in fact |
| and | moreover |
| another | not only X, but also Y |
| as well as | not to mention |
| besides that | other |
| further or furthermore | too |
| in addition or additionally | |

Not only will this course help you fulfill a graduation requirement, but it will also teach you skills you can utilize in a variety of fields.

In fact, I think you'll be surprised to learn just how often you think about this class long after you've fulfilled the requirements.

Math is a tremendously useful skill to master in order to manage your banking. Besides that, learning math will probably save you money in the long run by teaching you skills to prevent you from overpaying at stores or in restaurants, and when ordering that pizza with your fellow dormitory residents.

We'll touch on several areas of math, including some basic math such as addition, subtraction, multiplication, and division as well as more advanced skills such as fractions, ratios, and percentages.

*Pronunciation Note:* Addition signal words and phrases often occur at the beginning of a sentence. When speaking, pause where the comma would be in written English to add emphasis and let your listener know you have more information to add. You can also stress signal words by increasing your volume, slowing your speed, and raising the pitch of the signal words and phrases.

## Using Addition Signal Words and Phrases

Write a sentence giving two reasons or examples for each situation. Connect the ideas with an addition signal word or phrase.

1. examples of good study habits

   _____

   _____

2. examples of math classes everyone needs

   _____

   _____

3. examples of when you use math at school

   _____

   _____

4. reasons to form a study group

   _____

   _____

5. reasons to go to college

   _____

   _____

6. reasons to save money

   _____

   _____

Work with a partner. Each of you should read one of your sentences aloud and then respond by adding another reason or example to those given by your partner. Begin your response with an addition signal word or phrase.

**Analyzing the Situation**

Work with a partner. Read each situation and decide what you would say or do to express your reasons. Connect your ideas with signal words. Write a dialogue for each on a separate sheet of paper.

1. Your roommate wants to drop out of college.

   _____

   _____

2. Your study group wants to study from 10 PM to midnight at the library.

   _____

   _____

3. You friends want you to enroll in a dance class instead of Math for Everyday Life.

   _____

   _____

# Listening 1: A Course Introduction

**Listening for Information**

The listening passage is an excerpt from a math instructor's basic mathematics course introduction. The introduction explains why the math course is required in order to graduate from the university. During the introduction, the instructor gives many reasons to explain the university's rationale for requiring the math course. As you listen to the course introduction, complete this note-taking chart. The first row has been done for you.

| Topic | Tally (how many examples are given) | What are the examples? |
|---|---|---|
| Stigma | /// | math is challenging<br>people think math isn't related to discipline<br>people think math isn't needed for everyday life |
| Basic Concepts | | |
| Percentages | | |
| Conversions | | |
| Government Finances | | |
| Probability and Odds | | |

Listen again to the introduction. What addition signal words and phrases did you hear?

_____

_____

_____

_____

_____

Compare your list with a partner. Did your partner notice any words that you didn't?

## Speaking

### Repeating to Confirm Accuracy or Get More Information

Several strategies can be used to confirm you heard something accurately. You can form questions or repeat information.

---

One-Word Questions

*What?*

*Really?*

*Oh?*

*Where?*

| | |
|---|---|
| The meeting will be held in room 210. | Where? |
| The math class was the best I've ever taken. | Really? |

Auxiliary Questions

*You did?*

*They were?*

*You think?*

| | |
|---|---|
| I think everyone should take three math classes. | You think? |
| I went to the library for four hours last night. | You did? |

Repeat a Word or Phrase

| | |
|---|---|
| I'm taking four classes next semester? | Four classes? |
| I am going to go to the University of Wisconsin. | Wisconsin? |

Repeat a Line (or Part of a Line)

| | |
|---|---|
| My best teacher was my algebra teacher. | Your best teacher was your algebra teacher? |

*Pronunciation Note:* Each strategy requires rising intonation, meaning your voice rises or goes up at the end of the question. Ask your teacher to demonstrate the rising intonation.

---

## Discussing

Read these questions about good classes. In a few minutes, you will talk about these questions. To prepare for the discussion, write notes on the lines.

1. What is the best class you have ever taken? When did you take it? Where did you take it? Who was your teacher?

   _____

   _____

   _____

   _____

2. What made this class so good?

   _____

   _____

   _____

   _____

3. Can you make some general statements about what makes a class good? What are three or four qualities of a good class?

   _____

   _____

   _____

   _____

4. What did you learn in this class that you will use in your everyday life?

   _____

   _____

   _____

   _____

## Repeating

Work with a small group. Take turns asking each other the questions. When someone says something that is not clear or that you want more information about, use one of the strategies in the box on page 125. Compile your notes into a short summary about what makes a class good and what kind of content people use in everyday life.

_____

_____

_____

_____

_____

Based on what you learned in your group, what do your favorite classes have in common? What kind of information is used later in everyday life?

_____

_____

_____

_____

_____

## Making an Impromptu Speech

When it is your turn, your teacher will randomly select one of these course names. You will have two minutes to give examples of how this class is important in everyday life.

Course 1: Public Speaking

Course 2: English Composition

Course 3: Basic Mathematics

Course 4: General Science

Course 5: Introduction to [a second language]

Course 6: World History

# Part 2: Math in the Professional World

## Pre-Listening Activities

People choose their area of study for a variety of reasons. Sometimes they are following in the footsteps of a parent or mentor. Other times they choose an area they feel passionately about. Still others may choose something because of what they like to study . . . or what they want to avoid studying. People who don't enjoy working with numbers might follow a career path that doesn't involve math or the sciences. However, math is often a required subject regardless of the area of study. Answer these questions with a partner.

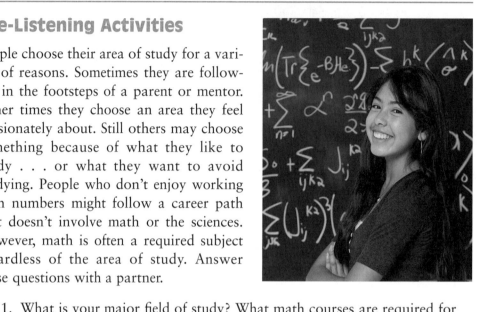

1. What is your major field of study? What math courses are required for you to be accepted into a university? What math courses are required for you to graduate?

   _____

   _____

   _____

2. List any careers that you think should not require math studies. List any careers that should require math courses. What makes math more applicable to one course of study over another?

   _____

   _____

   _____

3. Name as many kinds of math courses as you can. Which have you studied?

   _____

   _____

   _____

## Strategy: Listening for Key Words

Academic work sometimes requires you to think outside of the box, meaning to think about something traditional in a different way. Thinking outside the box allows you to be creative and unconventional. It gives you a new perspective. Discussions like this might have new vocabulary or ideas that will make it challenging to understand. When you listen to an academic discussion about new ideas, you need to concentrate on the key words. It is the key words that are usually the details.

The first thing to do is identify the purpose of the interaction. For example:

We need to discuss the types of math used in the field of medicine.

**Purpose: types of math required for doctors**

Then, take note of the details you should listen for. In other words, predict what content you should listen specifically for.

**Details: names of math courses**

By narrowing the details that you should concentrate on, you'll be more likely to catch the details.

Read this excerpt from a university medical school recruiter's answer to "What math courses are required for a medical student?" There are a lot of words, but these are only a few details you need to know.

> Our university has one of the premiere medical programs in the country. Because of the teaching hospital we have on campus, more math courses are required for a student of medicine than required for similar degrees at other universities. The same math courses as all disciplines are required: algebra, geometry, and advanced algebra. Beyond the basics, medical students are required to take trigonometry and calculus. Other courses are recommended, but those are based on what type of medicine you intend to study.

**Which details should you have noted?**

You should listen specifically for the name of math types or courses. In this case, you only need to write five details: algebra, geometry, advanced algebra, trigonometry, and calculus.

**Predicting Details**

Predict what kind of details you should note about these questions that might be heard during a discussion or lecture.

1.  What crimes are most prevalent on college campuses?
    General Idea:

    _____

    Details:

    _____

    _____

2.  What preventions should I take against contracting influenza?
    General Idea:

    _____

    Details:

    _____

    _____

3.  What are the costs I need to think about when going to a university?
    General Idea:

    _____

    Details:

    _____

    _____

4.  What majors are best suited for someone who excels in writing?
    General Idea:

    _____

    Details:

    _____

    _____

5. What careers are best suited for someone who excels in mathematics?

General Idea:

_____

Details:

_____

_____

 **Speaking**

## Brainstorming

In academic conversations and group discussions, you will sometimes have to think of a lot of ideas before narrowing down your choices and making the best selection. A good strategy is brainstorming. The goal of brainstorming is to generate a long list of possible ideas and is useful when thinking outside of the box.

---

STEPS

1. Make sure everyone knows the topic and writes it on the paper.

2. Offer any ideas no matter how different or unusual they seem.

3. Don't wait to be invited; just jump in!

4. Don't discuss any ideas at length; just add suggestions to the list.

5. Attempt to build off other suggestions.

6. Write quickly, focusing only the key words.

---

Note that brainstorming is about quantity and not quality. No suggestion is bad. Concentrate only on the key words so you begin to get the details.

## Brainstorming

Work in a small group. Brainstorm a list in response to each topic.

1. reasons to study math

   _____

   _____

   _____

2. reasons to know a second language

   _____

   _____

   _____

3. ways to make new friends

   _____

   _____

   _____

4. qualities every boss should have

   _____

   _____

   _____

# Listening 2: Brainstorming about Math in the Professional World

## Listening in Groups

Listen to the students brainstorm a list of ideas for a class presentation titled "Math in the Professional World." Discuss the questions in a small group.

## Focus on Language

1. What strategies are used to confirm information? Refer to the box in Part 1 on page 125.

   _____

   _____

2. List key words the students use during their brainstorming.

   _____

   _____

3. Do you think enough ideas are generated during the brainstorming session? Why or why not?

   _____

   _____

4. Write any phrases or idioms that you are not familiar with. Discuss what they mean and in what type of interactions they are appropriate.

   _____

   _____

## Focus on Tone

1. Describe the tone used by each member of the group.

   _____

   _____

2. Is each person's tone appropriate? Why or why not?

   _____

   _____

## Focus on Nonverbal Communication

1. What nonverbal cues are used to show how each member of the group feels about suggestions from other group members?

   _____

   _____

2. Were any of these inappropriate? Why or why not?

   _____

   _____

3. Which student do you think has the most expressive facial expressions? Does this positively or negatively affect the interaction?

   _____

   _____

## Summary

1. What brainstorming rules do the group members adhere to?

   _____

   _____

   _____

   _____

2. Are any brainstorming rules broken? If so, what were they? Speculate on why you think they were broken?

   _____

   _____

   _____

   _____

3. Which brainstorming idea do you like best? Why?

   _____

   _____

   _____

   _____

**You Be the Judge**

Parents are legally responsible for their children until they turn 18. What should that responsibility include? There are many opinions and ideas. Some families believe you care for children by providing housing and food. Others think the responsibilities are greater. In the United States, parents are responsible for making sure their children are educated. How much responsibility should a parent have for the children's education? Sometimes a case will become a legal issue. One case in Kentucky made the news.

Read this court case about a daughter who failed her math test.

The story begins with a 16-year-old daughter whose parents were divorced. Her father legally had custody of her, but she lived with her mother. The teenager began skipping classes at her high school and was truant. She had a baby. A court ordered her to earn her General Equivalency Diploma, or GED (a test you can take that is the equivalent of a high school, or secondary school, diploma). When she was 18, a legal adult, she started school. Four months into the program, she took the math test, but failed. As a result, she did not earn her GED as the court had ordered her to do. Because she failed, her father was sent to jail for 180 days for contributing to the delinquency of a minor because he was responsible for making sure his daughter received the GED.

Does the punishment fit the crime? If you were the judge, what would you do? Write two or three reasons for your decision.

---

---

---

---

What other alternatives would you consider for any of the parties involved (the mother, the father, or the daughter)?

---

---

---

---

Work with a small group. Discuss your decisions and your reasons. Come to a group consensus. What did you decide? Present your decisions to the rest of the class.

---

---

---

---

# Part 3: History of Mathematics

## Pre-Listening Activities

As discussed in Part 1, math is a part of everyday life; and in Part 2, math plays a role in careers beyond the sciences. Part 3 will discuss the role that math has played throughout history. Concepts used today in basic arithmetic, algebra, geometry, and other areas of mathematics have roots in history as far back as Babylonia, Mesopotamia, Egypt, and Greece. Although not as well known as other historical figures, there have been notable mathematicians who have made their mark in time. Answer these questions with a partner.

1. What do you know about the following mathematicians?
   * Euclid of Alexandria
   * Charles Babbage
   * Blaise Pascal
   * Pythagoras

   _____

   _____

   _____

2. Although math has roots in a variety of cultures and has been translated to and from other languages, some people claim math is the one universal language. Do you agree? Why or why not?

   _____

   _____

   _____

3. What role does math play in the 21st century? How has it changed since its inception in ancient history?

   _____

   _____

   _____

## Strategy: Listening for and Using Significance Signal Words and Phrases

Instructors often use signal words and phrases to let you know when they are emphasizing an important point. Listening for these signal phrases that denote significance will help you recognize what should be written in your notes. Phrases indicating significance are often a combination of nouns and adjectives and/or adverbs.

| Adjectives | Adverbs | Nouns |
|---|---|---|
| *important* | *especially* | *change* |
| *key* | *substantially* | *event* |
| *main* | *quite* | *issue* |
| *major* | *very* | *point* |
| *notable* | | *reason* |
| *primary* | | *result* |
| *significant* | | |
| *vital* | | |

Adjective + Noun Combinations

*a key problem*

*a major issue*

*a notable event*

*a strong reason*

*a vital result*

*an important change*

Adverb + Adjective + Noun Combinations

*especially noteworthy point*

*notably different characteristic*

*quite relevant problem*

*substantially influential moment*

*very important concept*

## Practicing Significance Signal Phrases

Think of five more adjectives, adverbs, and nouns to add to the list. Then share them with a small group.

| Adjectives | Adverbs | Nouns |
|---|---|---|
| _____ | _____ | _____ |
| _____ | _____ | _____ |
| _____ | _____ | _____ |
| _____ | _____ | _____ |
| _____ | _____ | _____ |

# Reading

Read the short article on the basic ideas of algebra from the National Aeronautics and Space Administration.

## (M-1) Algebra—the basic ideas

Don't expect here a full-blown course on high-school algebra; it cannot be done, not in such limited space. These are just the bare bones—just three basic ideas and rules for handling relations ("equations") involving **unknown quantities** whose values you are trying to find.

In most calculations you try to find a **number**. For instance, the area of a rectangular plot of land 25 meters long and 40 meters wide (or yards, or feet) is

$$25 \times 40 = 1000 \text{ square meters}$$

Until the multiplication is carried out, we may represent the answer by some letter, usually $x$, and write

$$25 \times 40 = x$$

One can then say "$x$ stands for the **unknown quantity**". The fundamental idea of algebra is very simple:

> **The unknown quantity $x$ is a number like any other. It may be added, subtracted, divided or multiplied in any way appropriate for ordinary numbers.**

A mathematical relationship involving known numbers (like 25 or 40) and unknown ones (like $x$) is known as an **equation**. Often $x$ is not given as cleanly as above, but is buried inside some complicated expression. To get a solution, one must replace the given equation (or equations) with others, containing the same information but cleaner in appearance. The final goal is to **isolate** the unknown, to make it stand apart ("isola" is island in Italian), to bring the equation to the above form, namely

> **$x$ = (expression containing only known numbers)**

Once that form is reached, the number which $x$ represents can be quickly calculated. For instance:

> **"What is the number which, if you double it, then add 5**
> **and divide the sum by 3, you get 3?"**

Call that number $x$. The information stated here in words can also be written down in equation form:

$$(2x + 5)/3 = 3$$

Parentheses here enclose quantities handled like a single number, and 2x means "2 times $x$." In algebra, **symbols** (or parentheses) **standing next to each other** are understood to be **multiplied**. If you stick to this rule, you will never be confused by the similarity between the letter $x$ and the multiplication sign. Computer programs, by the way, usually represent multiplication by *, placed a little lower than here.

---

A second fundamental idea in algebra is:

> **If you have an equation and modify both its sides in *exactly the same way*,**
> **what you get is *also* a valid equation.**

You may **add**, **subtract**, **multiply** or **divide** any number you wish; as long as it's done equally to both sides of the equality, the result is still valid. Also, the new equation still contains the same information as before. (But don't multiply both sides by 0 and get 0 = 0; the result **is** correct, but all your information has now vanished into thin air.)

For example, the equation given earlier:

$$(2x + 5)/3 = 3$$

Multiply both sides by 3:

$$(2x + 5) = 9$$

Subtract 5 from both sides:

$$2x = 9 - 5 = 4$$

Divide both sides by 2:

$$x = 4/2 = 2$$

and you have the result, $x = 2$. High school algebra contains a good deal more, but the above simple rules, plus the basic goal "isolate the unknown number," will get you a long way.

One last step is frequently skipped, but should not be. **Just to make sure** you haven't made a mistake along the way, take the **original** equation

$$(2x + 5)/3 = 3$$

replace in it the unknown quantity $x$ by the value you have derived—in this case, by the number 2—and check whether the two sides are indeed equal. If they are, you can rest assured that your answer is correct.

---

A third element is **substitution**:

**If you know that an unknown quantity or expression can be expressed in a different way, you may substitute in its place the alternative way of expressing it. This gives a new equation, which sometimes leads to the solution.**

Suppose you have two unknown quantities, **x** and **y**, and two equations linking them (two are needed to get a unique solution—with just one, an infinite number of pairs of **x** and **y** exist that satisfy it):

$$x + 2y = 7 \qquad (1)$$
$$2x + y = 5 \qquad (2)$$

Subtract **2y** from both sides of (1):

$$x = 7 - 2y \qquad (3)$$

and substitute this for **x** in (2)

$$2(7 - 2y) + y = 5$$

Then

$$14 - 4y + y = 5$$

Subtract 14

$$-4y + y = 5 - 14$$
$$-3y = -9$$

Multiply both sides by (-1)

$$3y = 9$$
$$y = 3$$

Then from (3)

$$x = 7 - 2y = 7 - 6 = 1$$

As a final test, put **x=1, y=3** in equations (1) and (2) and make sure that these solutions indeed satisfy the requirement. If they don't you probably made a mistake somewhere along the way.

**Another type of substitution**, namely substituting entire equations, is postponed to the end of section (M-3), which is about **formulas**.

*Dr. David P. Stern*

From National Aeronautics and Space Administration, www-spof.gsfc.nasa.gov/stargaze/Salgeb1.htm. Accessed on February 1, 2010.

## Identifying and Inserting Significance Signal Phrases

Imagine you had to tutor someone on the basic concepts of algebra. Answer these questions. Then compare your answers with a partner.

1. Using the reading on pages 141–44, highlight the signal phrases inserted.

2. As a tutor, where would you add other significance signal words? Mark the spots with arrows.

3. What signal phrases would you choose? Insert them in the text.

**Vocabulary Power**

There are a number of terms and phrases in this lecture that you may encounter in other academic settings. Add at least five vocabulary items to your vocabulary notebook or log.

Match the words in bold from the lecture on the left with a definition on the right.

1. _____ . . . math, itself, hasn't really changed throughout history, but it has been studied and new discoveries about existing mathematical concepts have **evolved**.

2. _____ While credit needs to be **attributed** to the Babylonian and Egyptian mathematicians that preceded the Greeks . . .

3. _____ . . . the word *mathematics* is **derived** from the Greek language and it means "subject of instruction."

4. _____ The Thales Theorem **orders** that an angle within a semicircle is a right angle.

5. _____ Other major contributions from Greek mathematicians include the **fundamentals** of geometry, important ideas related to number theory, and applied mathematics.

6. _____ . . . Galileo used math to make **strides** in astronomy . . .

7. _____ Another name you'll know is Isaac Newton who **capitalized** on the work Keplar had done, combined it with his own studies, and created a new study.

8. _____ The main thing to remember about this time period is that math moved from being a **concrete** study to having a distinctive quality of abstractness.

a. specifies with authority

b. originated

c. progress

d. given

e. firm, solid

f. basic ideas

g. took advantage of

h. changed

## Note-Taking Strategy: Borrowing Someone Else's Notes

Sometimes it helps to meet with a classmate to compare notes. You might find important details that you missed. First, you need to take the best notes you can.

## Listening 3: Highlights in Mathematic History

### Taking Notes

The listening passage is a lecture from a mathematics class. The instructor is discussing the history of mathematics and how events have shaped what the field of mathematics has become in today's modern world. Take notes as you normally would as you listen to the lecture. Pay special attention to significance signal phrases since these are often followed by important details you should note. Write your notes in the space provided.

| | |
|---|---|
| ○ | |
| | |
| | |
| | |
| | |
| ○ | |
| | |
| | |
| | |
| | |

A set of notes is shown for the mathematics lecture you will hear. The student wrote the significance signal words (or an abbreviation for them) on the left side of the page and the details on the right side. Look at the notes. Then answer the questions.

| | | | |
|---|---|---|---|
| | | most important note | math hasn't altered, has evolved |
| ○ | | 3 notable texts | between 1600 and 1900 B.C. 2 in Egypt |
| | | most interesting contributions | Greeks |
| | | esp. memorable mathematicians | Thales Pythagoras |
| | | major concepts | Theorem of Thales Pythagorean Theorem |
| | | other major contributions | geometry number theory |
| ○ | | a significant geographic region | applied math China |
| | | a key feature | decimals |
| | | key players in Mid. Ages | Fibonacci Bradwardine |
| | | one of the most important time periods | 17th cent. |
| | | main thing to remember about 18th + 19th cent. | abstract |
| | | final point | 20th cent. |

1.  How do your notes compare to the student's notes?

    _____

    _____

    _____

2.  Who did a better job at catching the signal phrases? Who did a better job at writing details?

    _____

    _____

    _____

3.  What would you add to your notes? What would you add to the other student's notes? Add any details you think the student is missing. Transfer details from their notes into yours. Highlight the differences.

    _____

    _____

    _____

4.  What advantages are there to comparing notes with a classmate? Are there disadvantages? Explain.

    _____

    _____

    _____

**Checking Your Understanding: Main Ideas**

Review your notes. Listen again to the lecture again if necessary, and then put a check mark (✓) next to the statements that best reflect the main ideas.

_____ Basic mathematical changes have taken place over time, but new discoveries have not altered the history of math.

_____ Credit needs to be given to the early and later mathematicians more so than those from the Middle Ages.

_____ New discoveries have evolved from existing mathematical concepts from the earliest to the most recent times.

_____ Early math has progressed in such a way that it has led to modern-day degrees and careers.

_____ The main thing to remember is that math has progressed from abstractness to concreteness.

**Checking Your Understanding: Details**

Use your notes, and put a check mark (✓) next to the best answers. Some questions have more than one answer.

1. Where were notable texts written during the early days of mathematics?

   a. _____ Greece

   b. _____ Babylonia

   c. _____ Egypt

   d. _____ Iraq

2. Who were memorable Greek mathematicians?

   a. _____ Thales of Miletus

   b. _____ Thales of Samos

   c. _____ Pythagoras of Miletus

   d. _____ Pythagoras of Samos

3. What is the premise of the Theorem of Thales?

   a. _____ $a^2 + b^2 = c^2$

   b. _____ the fundamentals of geometry

   c. _____ angles within semicircles are right angles

   d. _____ number theory

4. What is interesting about the evidence from China's contribution to mathematics?

   a. _____ It started during the Shang Dynasty.

   b. _____ A lot of evidence points to the fact that decimals began there.

   c. _____ Notations were written during this period.

   d. _____ Documentation was not recorded on paper.

5. Who is responsible for part of Isaac Newton's contributions to mathematics?

   a. _____ Galileo

   b. _____ Keplar

   c. _____ Brahe

   d. _____ Bradwardine

## Discussion

In the video, the students brainstormed a list of ideas for a presentation on a career that uses math titled "Math in the Professional World." Follow the brainstorming rules, and work with a small group to brainstorm your own list of ideas for a presentation with the same title.

Our List:

_____

_____

_____

_____

_____

Next, work with your group to weigh the pros and cons of each item on your brainstorming list. Continue narrowing your list until you agree on one topic. Review the information on discussing pros and cons on page 55 and on using persuasion on page 88.

Our Topic:

_____

Last, talk about the details you would include in your presentation. What would be your central idea, your key points, and your significant details? Present your final idea to the class and include signal phrases to indicate what you want to highlight.

_____

_____

_____

_____

_____

# Rapid Vocabulary Review

From the three answers on the right, circle the one that best explains, is an example of, or combines with the vocabulary item on the left as it is used in this unit.

| Vocabulary | Answers | | |
|---|---|---|---|
| Synonyms | | | |
| 1. the odds | the success | the probability | the differences |
| 2. stick to | listen to | point to | adhere to |
| 3. delve into | investigate | divide | coincide |
| 4. inception | a new idea | a disagreement | a beginning |
| 5. prevalent | famous | common | in good condition |
| 6. traditional | common | innovative | fresh |
| 7. precede | come before | study in detail | begin in a place |
| 8. insight | additions, bonuses | books, reports | opinions, ideas |
| 9. go out on a limb | do something fast | meet with a person | take a risk |
| 10. alter | change | organize | employ |
| 11. desirable | needed | wanted | seen |
| 12. fulfill | reject | complete | differ |
| Combinations and Associations | | | |
| 13. excel ___ math | for | in | on |
| 14. narrow ___ a topic | down | off | on |
| 15. a career ___ | street | path | way |
| 16. stem ___ an old problem | by | from | up |
| 17. fasten ___ | your seatbelt | your ideas | your vacation |
| 18. related ___ | to | from | of |
| 19. chip __ on a gift | off | in | by |
| 20. touch __ a topic | for | in | on |

## ⇨⤬⤐ Synthesizing: Projects and Presentations

| Short In-Class Speaking Assignments | Longer Outside Assignments |
|---|---|
| The First Class | Researching a Well-Known Contributor to a Field of Study |
| Talk about the first class you have to take in the field of study you want to pursue. State the name of the class, some of its content, and why it's important to take this class and how it will be helpful after you've found a job in your field. | Choose a famous person who made some impact on the modern world of your field of study. Prepare a presentation on that person's life and contributions. Prepare a short presentation for your classmates. Include significance signal phrases throughout so your audience will be aware of what you think are the most important details. Be prepared to answer questions. Consider using visual aids to enhance your presentation. |
| Top Ten List | Teach a Mathematics Lesson |
| Work with a small group to brainstorm the top ten reasons everyone should love mathematics. Present your list to the rest of the class. | Work with a group and choose one of the following basic math concepts: addition, subtraction, multiplication, or division. Imagine math is a second language and many people don't speak it. Brainstorm a list of creative ways to teach the mathematical concept of your choice. Then narrow your teaching ideas to just one and write a math as a second language lesson. Teach the rest of the class. |

# Vocabulary Log

To increase your vocabulary knowledge, write a definition or translation for each vocabulary item. Then write an original phrase, sentence, or note that will help you remember the vocabulary item.

| Vocabulary Item | Definition or Translation | Your Original Phrase, Sentence, or Note |
| --- | --- | --- |
| 1. significant | important, having great meaning | important = daily language significant = academic language |
| 2. enthusiastic | | |
| 3. a stigma | | |
| 4. a dosage | | |
| 5. premiere | | |
| 6. custody | | |
| 7. premise | | |
| 8. a discipline | | |
| 9. evolve | | |
| 10. noteworthy | | |
| 11. capitalize on | | |
| 12. likely | | |
| 13. anticipate | | |
| 14. an overview | | |

| Vocabulary Item | Definition or Translation | Your Original Phrase, Sentence, or Note |
|---|---|---|
| 15. truant | | |
| 16. parties (in a contract) | | |
| 17. derived from | | |
| 18. the prospect | | |
| 19. outside the box | | |
| 20. a major (n.) | | |
| 21. major (adj.) | | |
| 22. prospect | | |
| 23. furthermore | | |
| 24. despite | | |
| 25. probability | | |

# 5 Sociology: Stratification

Sociology is a field that studies and classifies people into groups based on a variety of factors. Some of those factors can be controlled; others people are born with. Sociology attempts to understand human behavior and the groups and associations that humans form or are born into and explain the effects that they have on society as a whole.

# Part 1: Birth Order

## Pre-Listening Activities

Everyone is either a youngest, middle, oldest, or only child. No one can control the order in which they are born, yet some people believe birth order affects personality and behavior and, to some degree, can predict a person's best option for groups to join or careers to pursue. Answer these questions with a partner who has the same ranking in birth order as you.

1. Do you think that everyone with the same birth order has the same characteristics? Do you believe your personality traits are influenced by your birth order? Why or why not?

   _____

   _____

   _____

2. Are you a youngest, middle, oldest, or only child? Describe your personality.

   _____

   _____

   _____

3. Now switch partners and work with someone who has a different birth order ranking than you. Compare your personality traits. Are there any similarities? Differences? Create a Venn diagram from your discussion notes to share with the class.

   _____

   _____

   _____

## Strategy: Active Listening

In any interaction, you want to listen actively to understand the necessary information and to let the speaker know that you are listening and interested. There are several actions to take, and several actions to avoid when listening.

**DO**

> . . . pay attention to the other person

> . . . acknowledge the other person by nodding or smiling

> . . . make eye contact

> . . . give verbal cues such as *yes* or *right*

> . . . respond when necessary

> . . . ask clarification questions

*Pronunciation Note:* When asking clarification questions, use rising intonation.

**DON'T**

> . . . become distracted by other people or noises

> . . . interrupt

> . . . be disrespectful of the speaker's opinion

> . . . start thinking about what you will say next

> . . . lose focus

> . . . do other things while you are listening

## Active Listening

Line up with half of the class facing the other half of the class. Face your partner and talk about your birth order and your personality traits. Your partner will actively listen and ask clarification questions. Then switch roles. Answer the questions with your partner when the activity is complete.

1. How many items from the DO list did you do actively? Which were easier than others?

   _____

   _____

   _____

2. What made this activity challenging?

   _____

   _____

   _____

3. What can you do to overcome challenges when listening?

   _____

   _____

   _____

 ## Listening 1: Birth Order and Careers

### Listening for Information

The listening passage is a conversation between an instructor and a student. They are discussing the influence that birth order has on career choices and a sociological research project that the student may work on. As you listen to the conversation, write answers to the questions.

1. What does the instructor want to pursue studies in?

   *personality make career success, make career makes career successful*

2. Is the oldest child the most intelligent?

   *Yes.*

3. What type of careers might an oldest child drift toward?

   *Doctor, lawyer*

4. Why might a youngest child become an actor?

   *Creative*

5. What personality traits might a middle child possess?

   *less selfish than younger, make more people happy*

6. To whom might only children resemble?

   *First child –*

## Speaking

### Paraphrasing

Sometimes the listener will want to make sure they understand or help with the clarification process by paraphrasing—using other words—to explain what the speaker said. Paraphrasing keeps the speaker's original meaning, but might make the words easier to understand. Some phrases you can use to let the original speaker and the listener know you are paraphrasing are:

> *I think what you meant was . . .*
>
> *You're saying . . . Is that right?*
>
> *You said that . . ., correct?*
>
> *If I understood you correctly, your point is that . . .*
>
> *Let me make sure I understand. You believe . . .*
>
> *What you are saying is . . .*
>
> *Let me see if I got that.*

### Paraphrasing

Read these statements from the conversation. Paraphrase them so that you keep the speaker's main ideas, but you use different words in order to make sure you understand.

1. Not only does birth order seemingly affect personality, it seems to affect salary.

   *Birth order is likely to influence [~~personality~~] Character and ~~salary~~ income*

2. I want to do an in-depth study to see if these first-borns tend to drift toward certain disciplines more than others.

   *I prefer to do a thorough research to see if [the oldest children] has tendency to older . . .*

3. Was it because they've spent a lifetime acting in a quest to get attention from their parents and older siblings?

   _____

   _____

## Role-Playing

Work with two classmates to role play possible conversations for this situation. Use the phrases in the box on page 161 or others that you can think of to write dialogues. Then exchange roles. Read your dialogues to the class.

SITUATION

Three students are discussing famous people and their careers. Talk about personality traits your famous person exhibits and how those personality traits make them successful at the career path they've followed.

Person A begins by making a statement.

Person B will ask for clarification about Person A's statement.

Person A will clarify and use other words.

Person C will paraphrase and then agree or disagree.

Person A:

_____

Person B:

_____

Person A:

_____

Person C:

_____

Can you extend the conversation with other ideas, clarifications, paraphrases, and statements of agreement and disagreement?

_____

_____

_____

_____

_____

## Making an Impromptu Speech

Each student will have two minutes to talk about his or her own birth order and how it will help . . . or hurt the career path being followed.

*sustainable*

# Part 2: Emphasizing Ideas

## Pre-Listening Activities

As you heard in Part 1, birth order is something we have no control over, yet some people believe it can, to some degree, affect our success. In Part 2, you will listen to some students discuss human behavior, the actions or reactions humans have to other things, and what factors affect it. Answer these questions with a partner.

1. List some acceptable behaviors that a person can exhibit in each of these settings/situations. Are there any behaviors that are unacceptable? Why are they unacceptable?

   a business meeting        a lunch with friends
   a classroom               a political rally
   a family dinner           an appointment with an advisor

   _____

   _____

   _____

2. Are there behaviors that are acceptable in one place but unacceptable in another? Give examples.     *He be serious in meeting*
   *acceptable: drink water, communication*        *be relax in party*
   *unacceptable: ~~eat~~ sleep, ~~stet~~ use mobile.*

   _____

   _____

3. Who or what determines which behaviors are acceptable and which aren't?
   *Regulation*

   _____

   _____

4. What factors affect human behavior?

   _____

   _____

   _____

## Strategy: Listening for and Emphasizing Ideas

Human behavior is the way people conduct themselves. It's often influenced by such things as culture, beliefs, personality, feelings, morals, social norms, and genetics. The way we act or the things we say in some discussions are influenced by these things as well. When someone feels strongly about something, there are some phrases you can use to make that clear, and you can listen for signals.

**Stress or emphasize content words.**

> I'm saying that all people should vote for a person based on the candidate's qualifications, and not on their own personal feelings.

**Pause before and after key words.**

> I'm saying that [pause] all [pause] people should vote for a person based on the candidate's [pause] qualifications [pause], and [pause] not [pause] on their own personal feelings.

> I'm saying that all people [pause] should [pause] vote for a person based on the candidate's [pause] qualifications [pause], and not on their own personal [pause] feelings [pause].

**Change your pitch or tone.**

> I'm saying that all people should vote for a person based on the candidate's qualifications, and not on their own personal feelings.

**Use nonverbal communication.**

gestures

facial expressions

posture

## Listening for and Emphasizing Ideas

Read the statements from the box on page 164 applying the strategy to the italicized words to a partner. Practice the ones that are the most challenging. Then write your own sentences about human behavior that should or should not take place at school. When you finish, read your sentences to a partner and employ at least one strategy in each. Try to use more than one strategy in several sentences. Write which strategies you think your partner is using. Then answer the questions on page 166.

1. _____

_____

_____

2. _____

_____

_____

3. _____

_____

_____

4. _____

_____

_____

5. _____

_____

_____

1. Was my partner able to identify which strategies I was using?

   _____

   _____

2. Which were my strongest? Which can I still improve?

   _____

   _____

3. Are there different words I should choose to emphasize? Which ones?

   _____

   _____

4. Rewrite one sentence and emphasize your ideas by choosing different
   strategies.

   _____

   _____

## Speaking

### Using Fillers

Written language and spoken language are very different. In written language, we use complete sentences that are grammatical. We have time to choose our words carefully. Spoken language is different. In spoken language, we sometimes repeat a word before we continue. Sometimes we don't finish a complete sentence before starting another one. One big difference between spoken and written language is that we use words or phrases that allow us more time to think of what we will say next. These are called fillers because they fill the spaces in the conversation when the speaker needs more time to think. Spoken language that has too many fillers may sound weak; however, in normal conversations and discussions, most people use fillers.

FILLERS

| | |
|---|---|
| *gee* | *I guess* |
| *I mean* | *oh* ✓ |
| *uh* | *uhm* ✓ |
| *well* | *yeah* |
| *yes* | *you know* ✓ |
| *you see* | *mmm* ✓ |

**Using Fillers**

Write three questions to ask a partner. Try to think of creative questions that the person will not be expecting. When you answer your partner's questions, insert fillers as needed.

1. _____

2. _____

3. _____

## Improvizing

When it is your turn, act out one of these scenarios.

1. Cancel a date with a young man or woman.

2. Explain to your teacher why your research paper is not finished.

3. Explain to the police officer why you were speeding.

4. Give a reason to your advisor about why you want to change classes.

5. Talk to your brother about why it's not a good idea for him to quit school.

6. Instruct a classmate on how to listen actively.

7. Share your reasons for choosing to learn English.

# Listening 2: Emphasizing Ideas

## Listening in Groups

Listen to the students talk about human behavior and what factors affect it. Discuss the questions in a small group.

## Focus on Language

1. What fillers are used? Why do you think they are used?

   _emm, I mean I I I Yes_
   _for thinking and guessing, and be not o sure, be sure_

2. Are enough verbal strategies used by each student to emphasize what he or she thinks is important?

   _Yes,_

   _norm=rule_

3. In your opinion, are enough paraphrasing phrases used?

   _Yes_

   _Coercion_
   _强迫_

4. Write any phrases or idioms that you are not familiar with. Discuss what they mean and in what type of interactions they might be appropriate.

*tight*

### Focus on Tone

1. Which student do you think does the best job of stressing key words and changing his or her tone to emphasize his or her ideas?

   *Number → Student 2.*

2. Are enough pauses used with stress and tone?

   *Yes.*

3. Based on the information in the box on page 164, what does each student need to do, if anything, to improve?

   *They should pauses in some part of sentence.*

   *non-Verbal communication*

### Focus on Nonverbal Communication

1. What nonverbal cues are used to show active listening? List suggestions for improvement.

   *Shake hand.   n-  face to. Listener.*

2. What nonverbal cues are used to emphasize key words? List suggestions for improvement.

   *Change pitch*

3. Which student do you think has the most expressive facial expressions? Does this positively or negatively affect the interaction?

   *The man*

**Summary**

1. Which student is the best active listener? Who is the worst? Give reasons for your opinions (see page 158).

   <u>student 2          student 3</u>

   <u>Because</u>

2. Do you think anyone uses too many or too few fillers? How do their use or absence impact the interaction?

3. Is there one student you agree with more than the others? Why?

**You Be the Judge**

Throughout history, students have been expelled or discharged from school for a variety of behaviors.

Read this court case about a student who was discharged from school.

> In 2007, a young man was expelled from his high school for a period of six months for being involved in a fight on school grounds. The young man's mother filed a suit stating that six months exceeded the time limit in the school's conduct policy and that the policy is inefficient, unfair, and defective. The policy states that a student can be expelled for up to 80 days for a physical assault on any staff member, student, or school district associate. The policy also states that the student can be expelled for a year if the student has a weapon. The school board and the superintendent of schools claim that this student was expelled for six months because of the school district's zero-tolerance policy for fighting. The mother's suit asked for an unspecified amount of money for compensation.

1. If you were the judge, would you let the young man back in school? Write two or three reasons for your decision.

   Yes. Because he's young, if he can realize his falus, he should get a chance to ~~take~~ back school, ~~because~~ his mother paid some money for compensation

2. Would you be willing to grant monetary compensation to the young man and his mother? Why or why not?

   No, ~~Yes, because her son do something wrong, the mother should be responsible for it~~

3. Work with a small group. Discuss your decisions and your reasons. Come to a group consensus. What did you decide? Present your decisions to the rest of the class.

# Part 3: Social Stratification

## Pre-Listening Activities

Social stratification is the arrangement or divisions of people within a society. Divisions vary from culture to culture and society to society. The divisions create a hierarchy for a society. Who falls into the top, or bottom, of the hierarchy is often affected by factors such as race and gender. A person's membership with a certain group or rank in the hierarchy sometimes predicts his or her chances for success. Part 3 will focus on one facet of social stratification—class. Answer these questions with a partner.

1. What factors affect social standing in Western culture? Write any you can think of.

   _____

   _____

   _____

2. Which factors may negatively affect a person's place in society? Which might positively affect placement?

   _____

   _____

   _____

3. What are the factors that determine a person's class?

   _____

   _____

   _____

4. Do you believe a person's success is based on where he or she was born into society? Why or why not? Can you think of any examples of people who rose from a lower class to a higher class? Can you think of anyone who has fallen from a higher class to a lower class?

   _____

   _____

   _____

# Reading

One factor that may affect a person's social standing is gender. Read this article about women and equal rights in the United States. Discuss how gender status has changed throughout history.

## Women and Equal Rights

*Women marching for the right to vote, April 5, 1917.*

Women's status during America's grand experiment as the world's first democracy has undergone dramatic changes over the generations. The religious doctrine, written laws, and social customs that colonists brought with them from Europe asserted women's subordinate position. Women were to marry, tend the house, and raise a family. Education beyond basic reading and writing was unusual. When a woman took a husband she lost what limited freedom she might have had as a single adult. Those few married women who worked for pay could not control their own earnings. Most could neither buy nor sell property or sign contracts; none could vote, sue when wronged, defend themselves in court, or serve on juries. In the rare case of divorce, women lost custody of their children and any family possessions.

During the Revolutionary War, women contributed in virtually every capacity, from doing fieldwork at home to fighting on battlefields. But their pleas for rights under the new democracy were disregarded. Women actually lost legal ground as a result of the new United States Constitution.

Sixty years later, in July 1848, a small group of women set about to change their second-class status. They launched a peaceful revolution that has since encircled the globe—the Women's Rights Movement. At the convention they held in Seneca Falls, New York, 68 women and 32 men signed a Declaration of Sentiments and Resolutions. It described 18 areas of life where women's rights were denied and demanded an end to women's inferior status.

Opposition arose immediately, but these new pioneers had proposed a magnificent new America. Reformers began speaking passionately for women's equality in small-town forums and city halls. Annual women's rights conventions drew tremendous crowds. In time, no aspect of public life would remain untouched by this second women's revolution.

Educational opportunities improved slowly as secondary schools, then colleges, were established for women. With the advent of coeducational schools, policies still limited women's admissions, financial assistance, course or program choices, and participation in activities. In the paid workforce, the situation was comparable. In the few occupations that were open to women, they were paid far less than men. Leadership in the major religions was not deemed to be women's province. Professions other than writing, school teaching, and nursing remained essentially closed to women as the 20th century opened.

By 1869, securing the right to vote became the primary focus of the Women's Rights Movement. For the next two generations, activists carried out a ceaseless campaign using every strategy imaginable, from leaflets and massive petition drives to street-corner speeches, legislative lobbying, and enormous street parades. Finally, on August 26, 1920, the Nineteenth Amendment to the U.S. Constitution was ratified. With it, 17 million women won for themselves that most basic promise of democracy: the right to vote.

Once the vote was achieved, many activists withdrew to pursue private interests. With the exceptions of nontraditional work opportunities during the two World Wars, women's position improved little over the next four decades.

The civil rights movements of the 1960s inspired a second wave of fervent activism confronting the inequities women faced in virtually all areas of American life. In communities everywhere, women worked on grassroots projects like battered women's shelters and rape crisis hotlines, child care centers, and health clinics. Commissions on the Status of Women investigated and reported on women's needs. State and federal laws were passed outlawing discrimination in employment and education, and women responded to their new opportunities with enthusiasm.

Today, America is living the legacy of the great progress women have made in all the areas addressed at the Seneca Falls Convention, while their earnest quest for full and true equality continues.

Mary Ruthsdotter

Projects Director, National Women's History Project

From National Park Service, www.nps.gov/history/nr/travel/pwwmh/equal.htm. Accessed on February 1, 2010.

## Strategy: Identifying Redundancy or Restatements

Redundancy and restating are two ways to identify what an instructor thinks is important. If he or she mentions it more than once, it is probably important enough to write in your notes. There are some key words and phrases that indicate when a main point, detail, or example is being repeated. The most obvious signal is when an instructor uses the exact same words or repeats part of a longer phrase or sentence.

> The two sociologists completed the experiment on different populations, but came to the exact same conclusions. Different populations, the exact same conclusions. Regardless of the fact that many people do not move from one social class to another, most people still believe it is possible to achieve the American Dream.

### Words or Phrases that Precede a Redundancy or Restatement

*another term is*                *the longer version is*

*in other words*                 *to explain it differently*

*in short*                       *to say it another way*

*let me repeat that*             *to word it more simply*

Most people still believe that the American Dream can be pursued and achieved with skill and effort. In other words, they think the American Dream can come true if you work hard.

Working hard will enable a person to move from a lower class to a higher class and not remain bound into the class he or she was born. And, although not as likely, a person can fall from a higher class to a lower class due to a job loss, an illness, or some other unfortunate twist of fate. In short, it is possible to move to a new class. Up or down.

## Using Redundancy and Restatements

Read the statements from the reading on pages 175–77. Imagine you had to give a presentation on the information provided. Rewrite the statements to repeat or restate all or part of the statements to emphasize what you consider the most important part of the statement.

1. Most could neither buy nor sell property or sign contracts; none could vote, sue when wronged, defend themselves in court, or serve on juries.

   _____

   _____

   _____

2. During the Revolutionary War, women contributed in virtually every capacity, from doing fieldwork at home to fighting on battlefields. But their pleas for rights under the new democracy were disregarded. Women actually lost legal ground as a result of the new United States Constitution.

   _____

   _____

   _____

3. With the advent of coeducational schools, policies still limited women's admissions, financial assistance, course or program choices, and participation in activities.

   _____

   _____

   _____

4. For the next two generations, activists carried out a ceaseless campaign using every strategy imaginable, from leaflets and massive petition drives to street-corner speeches, legislative lobbying, and enormous street parades.

_____

_____

_____

5. Today, America is living the legacy of the great progress women have made in all the areas addressed at the Seneca Falls Convention, while their earnest quest for full and true equality continues.

_____

_____

_____

Choose your own statements from the reading that you feel contain main points worth repeating or restating and rewrite them.

6. _____

_____

_____

7. _____

_____

_____

Read the statements emphasizing the content words and signal phrases to draw focus to the points being repeated or restated.

# Note-Taking

## Strategy: Highlighting to Organize Ideas

After taking notes, it's a good idea to organize the ideas, especially if ideas weren't presented in order or examples were given later. A good way to do that is to highlight your notes soon after listening to the lecture.

### Steps

1. Highlight each main idea in a different color.

2. Read your notes again and highlight details for each main idea in the same color as its corresponding main idea.

3. Study the matching colors together or rewrite your notes into an outline or note-taking chart from which to study.

In the lecture, you'll have the chance to take notes and then highlight them accordingly.

### Organizing Ideas

Look at the list of main ideas and details from a lecture about sociology for new students. Highlight each main idea in a different color.

| | | |
|---|---|---|
| archival | family | psychology |
| areas of sociology | famous sociologists | religion |
| economics | Herbert Spencer | research methods |
| education | Max Weber | surveying |
| experimental | observation | W.E.B. Du Bois |

**Vocabulary Power**

There are a number of terms and phrases in this lecture that you may encounter in other academic settings. Add at least five vocabulary items to your vocabulary notebook or log.

Match the words in bold from the lecture on the left with a definition on the right.

1. ___d___ We mentioned that families have a hierarchy with certain personality traits some consider to be **based on** the order in which we are born.

2. ___f___ Status is related to **prestige** or the respect people receive.

3. ___h___ This meager number, however, has **immense** wealth, tremendous prestige, and a lot of power.

4. ___a___ She started in a lower class and worked her way up to the upper class through hard work and **determination**.

5. ___c___ They do, however, still carry much status and **wield** a fair share of power.

6. ___e___ We've **accounted for** about 88 percent of the population.

7. ___b___ _c_ They are primarily employed in blue-collar jobs, or to use another term, those who perform **manual labor**.

8. ___g___ . . . but this **trend** came to an end . . .

a. decision to work toward a desired goal

b. work requiring physical activity

c. have or possess

d. because of, dependent on

e. captured or included

f. importance or influence based on fame

g. tendency, current way

h. enormous

download       polyn

## Listening 3: Social Class

**Listening to a Lecture**

The listening passage is a lecture from a sociology class. The instructor is discussing social class and the factors that determine a person's placement in that place in the social hierarchy. Throughout the lecture, the instructor repeats key information or restates it in different words. Take notes on the main ideas and details you hear in the order in which you hear them. Then, highlight your notes following the steps listed in the box on page 181.

basedon —

fochs on class
  each class fn USA is responsible ,
    money , respect and power
            prestge .   what people have access to.
economic
money ,

upper class.      >percent   a lot of power, population ,
    Some   one-free . for example
    law class,    middle class , capital class .
        CEO, much money   last 10 percent   are a of sociology
        as middle class, 45%    um sociolog.
                          & working class ;
    capital class has   power .   1990s.       the same as middle class

Compare your notes with a partner. Did you capture the same main ideas and details? Did you highlight information the same way?

## Checking Your Understanding: Main Ideas

Review your notes. Listen again to the lecture if necessary, and then put a check mark (✓) next to the statements that best reflect the main ideas.

_____ Class is determined by three factors: wealth, prestige, and power.

___X__ There are five main classes in the United States: upper, upper middle, middle, working, and lower.

_____ People can and will climb the social mobility ladder.

_____ Depending on your class, buildings can be constructed based on your wealth, prestige, or power.

___X__ Less than 10 percent of the population holds the most wealth, prestige, and power.

___✓__ Most people believe that everyone is socially mobile.

## Checking Your Understanding: Details

Use your notes, and put a check mark (✓) next to the best answers. Some questions have more than one answer.

1. Which characteristics are ascribed?

   a. ___✓__ power

   b. ___✓__ wealth

   c. _____ gender

   d. _____ rank

   e. _____ race

2. Which two classes hold most of the wealth in the United States?

   a. ___✓__ upper

   b. ___✓__ upper middle

   c. _____ middle

   d. _____ working

   e. _____ lower

3. Into which two categories do most white and blue collar workers fall?

    a. _____ upper

    b. __✓__ upper middle

    c. _____ middle

    d. __✓__ working

    e. __✓__ lower

4. Which class may struggle with paying monthly food bills?

    a. _____ upper

    b. _____ upper middle

    c. _____ middle

    d. __✓__ working

    e. _____ lower

5. Which class socializes with others in the same class?

    a. _____ upper

    b. _____ upper middle

    c. __✓__ middle

    d. _____ working

    e. _____ lower

6. Who is proof that America is a socially mobile country?

    a. _____ Gates

    b. _____ Trump

    c. __✓__ Oprah

## Debate

Divide the class into two teams and think about whether or not the American Dream is achievable. Half of the class will argue that the American Dream can be achieved. The other half will argue that it cannot.

Topic: The American Dream: Reality or Still a Dream?

Pro or Con: _____

Choose one team member to give an introductory statement and one to give a closing statement. Divide the arguments evenly among the remaining team members. Be prepared to disagree and counter at least one point from the other team. Each statement, argument, and counterargument lasts for two minutes.

Follow this debate format:

> Pro team member gives an introductory statement on the topic to present/preview pro opinion
>
> Con team gives an introductory statement on the topic to present/preview con opinion
>
> Con team member delivers first argument
>
> Pro team member rebuts with counterargument
>
> Pro team member delivers next argument
>
> Con team member rebuts with counterargument
>
> Team members will continue exchanging arguments and rebuttals until all team members have delivered their arguments and counterarguments.
>
> Open discussion (10 minutes)
>
> Pro team member gives a closing statement/summary on pro team's argument
>
> Con team member gives a closing statement/summary on con team's argument

Team member giving introductory statement _____

Team member giving closing statement _____

Other arguments: _____

_____

_____

_____

_____

_____

### Preparing Individually

Think about the selected topic and then write two reasons that support the achievement of the American Dream and two that are against the idea. You need to think about both sides so that you can argue effectively against the other team. Take time to research true stories and statistics to better prepare your arguments.

Pro 1:

_____

_____

Pro 2:

_____

_____

Con 1:

_____

_____

Con 2:

_____

_____

Now work with your team. Take turns discussing your pros and cons. Your group should select the strongest pros and cons to use during the debate. Select arguments that you think will be difficult for the other team to disagree with. Also think about responses you can use to counter the other team's arguments.

Arguments:

_____

_____

_____

_____

_____

_____

Counterarguments:

_____

_____

_____

_____

_____

_____

## Rapid Vocabulary Review

From the three answers on the right, circle the one that best explains, is an example of, or combines with the vocabulary item on the left as it is used in this unit.

| 'Vocabulary | Answers | | |
|---|---|---|---|
| Synonyms | | | |
| 1. siblings | lawyers / doctors | brothers / sisters | boss / employees |
| 2. coercion | belief | determination | force |
| 3. cancel | call off | destroy | provoke |
| 4. rare | famous | common | unusual |
| 5. lofty | very low | in the middle | very high |
| 6. dictate | read | tell | listen |
| 7. Hold up! | Look! | Wait! | Listen! |
| 8. expel | exert | hesitate | push out |
| 9. deny | say no | say yes | say maybe |
| 10. due to X | X = the result | X = the receiver | X = the cause |
| 11. unfair | impossible | unjust | irregular |
| 12. defective | it has a problem | it is not popular | it costs too much |
| Combinations and Associations | | | |
| 13. undergo a ___ | change | con | equipment |
| 14. wield ___ | food | power | hospitals |
| 15. a rags to riches ___ | piece of furniture | human being | story |
| 16. as a ___ | result | fact | mistake |
| 17. lost ___ | ground | air | books |
| 18. manual ___ | television | labor | medicine |
| 19. a period ___ | by | down | of |
| 20. be willing ___ | up | to | out |

# ⫸ Synthesizing: Projects and Presentations

| Short In-Class Speaking Assignments | Longer Outside Assignments |
|---|---|
| My Group | Behavior Observation |
| Divide the class into four groups: oldest, middle, youngest, and only children. Prepare a list of personality traits you all share and explain why they apply to your birth order. Be prepared to debate whether or not birth order affects behavior. | Sit for 30 minutes in a location where you can observe people's behavior. This can be a laundromat, a restaurant, a new place to study, or any place of your choice. Choose two or three people to observe, and watch their actions and behavior. Write your observations in a notebook and then prepare a presentation for your classmates on what behaviors everyone had in common, which were different, and why you think each may be appropriate or inappropriate in this location. |
| Story Telling | Against All Odds |
| Choose a picture out of a book or magazine. Create a story about this person's ascribed characteristics and his or her behaviors. Include details about the person's location, actions, and life (why it is the way it is). Be creative! Before reading your story to the class, prepare which key words and ideas should be emphasized and decide which strategies will work best. | Find a true story of someone whose American Dream came true. What ascribed characteristics did they have that made achieving their dreams harder than those who are ascribed other characteristics? What traits did they have that made them beat the odds? Prepare a speech on your rags to riches story. Consider using visual aids to enhance your presentation. |

## Vocabulary Log

To increase your vocabulary knowledge, write a definition or translation for each vocabulary item. Then write an original phrase, sentence, or note that will help you remember the vocabulary item.

| Vocabulary Item | Definition or Translation | Your Original Phrase, Sentence, or Note |
|---|---|---|
| 1.  in-depth | very detailed | an in-depth report on the war |
| 2.  compensation | | |
| 3.  hierarchy | | |
| 4.  gender | | |
| 5.  virtually | | |
| 6.  to drift | | |
| 7.  scenario | | |
| 8.  enormous | | |
| 9.  plea | | |
| 10.  prestige | | |
| 11.  posture | | |
| 12.  a petition | | |
| 13.  a weapon | | |

| Vocabulary Item | Definition or Translation | Your Original Phrase, Sentence, or Note |
|---|---|---|
| 14. to exhibit | | |
| 15. background | | |
| 16. an only child | | |
| 17. inferior | | |
| 18. inefficient | | |
| 19. a shelter | | |
| 20. quest | | |
| 21. a ladder | | |
| 22. an assault (on) | | |
| 23. disregard | | |
| 24. status | | |
| 25. hierarchy | | |

# 6 Astronomy: Outer Space

Astronomy is a study housed in the science field that examines the physics, chemistry, and behavior of stars, planets, and other bodies in the universe beyond the Earth's atmosphere. As one of the oldest sciences, it has fascinated amateur star gazers and professional astronomers for years. This unit covers some discoveries and news from the long history of astronomy.

# Part 1: Amateur Astronomers

## Pre-Listening Activities

The field of astronomy has been graced with many famous astronomers from its earliest days through its more recent history. Claudius Ptolemy, Nicolaus Copernicus, and Galileo Galilei are responsible for such things as predicting eclipses, knowing Earth's placement in the solar system, and building better telescopes. Modern astronomers, including Carl Sagan and Edwin Hubble, are known for more scientific achievements, such as high temperatures on Venus, oceans on Jupiter's moons, and the discovery that the universe is expanding. However, amateur astronomers have contributed to the field of astronomy as well.

Answer these questions with a partner.

1. Talk about any famous astronomers you are familiar with. What are they best known for discovering or explaining?

   _____Galileo_____,_____discovering_-____

   _____

   _____

2. The primary difference between amateur astronomers and professional astronomers is that professionals are doing scientific research. What are some other differences between amateurs and professionals?

   __professional_____astronomers____can____explore____the____

   _____

   _____

3. Would you like to be an astronomer, amateur or professional? What is appealing about the field? What is unappealing?

   _____

   _____

   _____

## Strategy: Predicting What You Will Hear

Ask *Wh-* questions about the details.

> *Who* will be speaking?

Ask *Wh-* questions about the content.

> *What* will the speaker talk about?

Ask yes-no questions for specific information.

> *Is* the speaker going to talk about famous amateur astronomers?

> *Will* the speaker give information about discoveries by amateur astronomers?

*Pronunciation Note*: *Wh-* questions have a falling intonation. In other words, your intonation goes down at the end of the question. Yes-no questions, however, have a rising intonation.

### Writing Prediction Questions

Write four questions for your partner about his or her intended field of study. Two should be *wh-* questions and two should be yes-no questions. Ask your partner the questions, using the proper rising or falling intonation of English. Then change roles.

*Wh-* questions

_____

_____

Yes-no questions

__Do you_____

_____

# Listening 1: An Automated Recording

## Listening for Information

The listening passage is an automated recording at the city's science center. The science center sponsors science nights and a university student is interested in information about the next lecture on amateur astronomy. When he calls the science center, he receives the automated recording about the details and content of the lecture. Before you listen, write some questions predicting what kind of information you would expect to hear in an automated recording about the lecture on amateur astronomy.

*Wh-* questions

_____

_____

Yes-no questions

_____

_____

As you listen to the recording, answer these *wh-* and yes-no questions.

1. When will it be held? _6 Pm_____

2. Where specifically will the lecture take place? ___main lobby green hall___

3. Will there be refreshments? __No_____

4. Is the speaker going to talk about any well-known amateurs? __Yes___

5. Does the speaker intend to talk about equipment? __No_____

6. Will equipment be provided? __Yes_____

7. Why should attendees bring a sweater? _go out doors  after dark____

8. Is registration open? _____Yes_____

## Speaking

### Expressing Lack of Information

Sometimes you have to tell your audience that you don't have all the information you need to offer additional information or answer their questions. There are certain phrases you can use to express a lack of information. In formal or academic settings, more formal phrases should be used; however, when talking with your friends, more informal phrases can be used.

EXPRESSING LACK OF INFORMATION

| |
|---|
| *I'm sorry. I can't remember the details.* |
| *I apologize, but I don't have all the information I need to answer your question.* |
| *I'm afraid I don't know.* |
| *I'm not sure.* |
| *I wish I knew!* |
| *I don't have the information with me, but I can send it to you later.* |
| *I have no idea!* |
| *You got me!* |
| *I've forgotten.* |
| *I couldn't tell you.* |

Which phrases do you think are more formal? Less formal? Can you think of other phrases to express a lack of information?

Sometimes people will take a guess even if they don't have all the information. Those phrases should still include an expression letting the listeners know it is a guess.

TAKING A GUESS

| |
|---|
| *I'm not sure, but I think the answer is yes.* |
| *I'm not certain, but I remember the teacher saying that . . .* |
| *I can't be 100 percent sure, however, I believe . . .* |

## Taking a Survey

Survey three people outside of class, and write their answers to the questions in the first column. Take note of who you ask and what the response was. For example, was it a friend, another student, an instructor, or a customer at the cafeteria?

| Questions | Interviewee 1 | Interviewee 2 | Interviewee 3 |
|---|---|---|---|
| How many planets are there in the solar system? | | | |
| How big can a black hole grow? | | | |
| How much time does it take for a star to form? | | | |

## Discussing

Answer these questions, and then discuss your survey results with a partner.

1. Did the interviewees express a lack of information? What expressions did they use to indicate this?

_____

_____

_____

2. Do you think the person's age, status, or relationship to you affected their answer?

_____

_____

_____

3. Did any results surprise you? Why or why not?

_____

_____

_____

## Analyzing the Situation

Work with a partner. Read each situation, and decide what you would say or do to express your feelings. Use appropriate phrases to express lack of information or take a guess. Write a dialogue for each on a separate sheet of paper.

1. A new student needs to find a professor in the business school. You know the approximate location of the business school but not the exact directions.

2. A professor asks you to participate in a research project. The topic is not in your area of expertise.

3. Your English teacher asks you to correct the errors in your most recent composition. You're not sure what the errors are, and you have no idea how to fix them.

4. A new student at the international center has to figure out which papers to fill out to make sure the visa paperwork is in order. You think you know which visa application is necessary.

5. Your tutor wants you to do the next problem in the math homework on your own. You believe you know how to do it, but you would like to check after you finish.

## Making an Impromptu Speech

When it is your turn, your teacher will randomly select one of these questions. You will have two minutes to answer the question. If you aren't sure of the answer, admit a lack of information using an expression from the box on page 197 or from the survey results, and then make a guess using an expression from the box on page 198.

1. Name the planets in order from the closest to the sun to the furthest away. Which is the smallest and which is the largest?

2. Which planet has the most moons? Name the planet and its moons.

3. What materials are needed to make a new star?

4. Who invented the telescope? When do you think it was invented?

5. What are the chances of a meteor hitting Earth? What would happen if one does strike the planet?

6. How old is the sun? How many years before the sun burns out?

7. Is there life on other planets? Why do you think so?

8. How many space missions have there been? From which countries?

# Part 2: Discussing Priorities

## Pre-Listening Activities

The operation that has become known as the National Aeronautics and Space Administration (NASA) was established by U.S. President Dwight D. Eisenhower in 1958. It was President John F. Kennedy who set the target of sending a man to the moon before 1970 (the first man landed on the moon in the summer of 1969). Since then NASA has continued to plan and execute missions to space.

1. What memories do you have or what history do you know of space missions?

   _____

   _____

   _____

2. If you were to travel to space, where would you want to go? Why? Do you have any concerns about such a mission?

   _____

   _____

   _____

3. What do you think NASA's next mission should be?

   _____

   _____

   _____

## Strategy: Listening for and Using Hedges

Depending on the situation, people want to avoid making overly strong statements, overstating information, forcing their opinions on others, or making untrue claims. It also helps to avoid hurting someone's feelings. In English, this is called hedging. There are several strategies you should listen for or use when discussing certain topics so you can best evaluate how the speaker feels and make sure your statements are qualified and not too strong.

Add words to soften a statement.

*Perhaps* a different topic would make a more exciting presentation.

She *probably* has the better idea because she is considering the future.

I *sort of* believe that we should consider missions that haven't been completed yet.

Begin statements with words that indicate a distance from a firm answer or opinion.

*Well*, I guess I would agree with her ideas about new missions.

*Maybe* you're right about the discoveries being part of the presentation.

Choose verbs that are weaker to avoid overstating.

I *guess* his idea is solid.

I *suppose* that could be true.

Use modals to suggest uncertainty or probability.

I suppose his idea *might* be a good choice.

I think that her idea to talk about Mars *could* be interesting to the audience.

Add words to avoid making an untrue claim.

It *seems* this mission has *one of* the best results.

He *tends to* believe that newer missions will *contribute to* more to space exploration than older ones.

## Using Hedges

Answer the questions and use hedging words or phrases to avoid being too strong, overstating, forcing your opinion, making untrue claims, or hurting someone's feelings.

1. Who was the first man on the moon?

   _____

2. Where should astronauts next travel?

   _____

3. How much of a national budget should a country dedicate to space exploration? Why?

   _____

4. Is there life on other planets? Why do you think so?

   _____

5. Can men live on the moon?

   _____

# Speaking

## Discussing Priorities

In academic discussions and after a brainstorming session, you sometimes have to choose one of several good suggestions. When discussing your options, you have to say which you believe should be the most important. There are some words or phrases you can use to express your opinion about which option is the most important. After beginning with one of the phrases, make sure to follow it with a specific reason for your choice.

### DECLARING A PRIORITY

| |
|---|
| *It's my opinion that the most important point is Option A because . . .* |
| *The way I see it, we have to choose Option A because . . .* |
| *I strongly believe the point that should receive the highest consideration is Option A because . . .* |
| *I feel that Option A should get the highest priority because . . .* |
| *It's quite important to choose Option A because . . .* |
| *I think Option A is the clear winner because . . .* |
| *Nothing should take precedence over Option A because . . .* |

Occasionally, you have to disagree or reject someone else's suggestion. This should be done tactfully and with the proper tone of voice. It's helpful if you can offer a reason for your disagreement or rejection. There are several phrases you can use to begin your statements.

**REJECTING SOMEONE'S PRIORITY**

| |
|---|
| *I'm not sure that's the best choice because . . .* |
| *I'd rather not include that because . . .* |
| *I think that is not the strongest decision because . . .* |
| *I don't know that I'd choose the same thing because . . .* |
| *I'm not sure that'll work because . . .* |

## Prioritizing

Review the brainstorming technique on page 131. With a small group, brainstorm a list of possible space missions that NASA should plan and execute. Brainstorm for 10 minutes. List your ideas.

Ideas for NASA Missions

_____

_____

_____

_____

_____

_____

After time is called, discuss you ideas. State which you think is most important and why. Listen to suggestions and reasons, and then accept, express doubt, or reject suggestions until your group agrees on one mission that NASA should plan and execute. Be prepared to share your decision and your reason with the other groups.

Our Priority

_____

_____

_____

_____

# Listening 2: Discussing Priorities

## Listening in Groups

This section includes information on several space missions, both past and present, and their purposes. In the video, the students are discussing the missions and deciding which mission they should focus on for their class presentation. Listen to the students discuss the topic of space missions discussed in their astronomy class. Discuss the questions in a small group.

## Focus on Language

1. What phrases are used to express a lack of information? <u>Note</u>: Don't worry about writing exact words. How do these affect the interaction?

   _____

   _____

2. List any hedges or expressions indicating the student is taking a guess that you hear. <u>Note</u>: Don't worry about writing exact words. Why do you think they are used? Do you think there are too many or too few?

   _____

   _____

3. What phrases do you hear the students use to express what they considered the most important priorities? <u>Note</u>: Don't worry about writing exact words.

   _____

   _____

4. What phrases are used to express doubt about someone's idea? <u>Note</u>: Don't worry about writing exact words.

   _____

   _____

5. Write any phrases or idioms that you are not familiar with. Discuss what they mean and in what type of interactions they are appropriate.

   _____

   _____

## Focus on Tone

1. Describe the tone used by each member of the group.

   _____

   _____

2. Who is most formal? Most informal? State a reason for your opinion.

   _____

   _____

3. Is each person's tone appropriate? Why or why not?

   _____

   _____

## Focus on Nonverbal Communication

1. What nonverbal cues are used to show how each member of the group feels?

   _____

   _____

2. Are any of these inappropriate? Why or why not?

   _____

   _____

3. Which student do you think has the most expressive facial expressions? Does this positively or negatively affect the interaction?

   _____

   _____

4. Do the nonverbal cues match the tone and word choice?

   _____

   _____

**Summary**

1. Who do you think represented himself or herself the best during the interaction? What language, tone, and nonverbal evidence can you use to support your choice?

   _____

   _____

   _____

2. Whose priority do you agree with? Why?

   _____

   _____

   _____

3. Whose ideas would you want to reject? Why? What words would you choose to state your reason?

   _____

   _____

   _____

4. Is there anyone you would not want to work with? Why?

   _____

   _____

   _____

# You Be the Judge

In Units 1–5, you had an actual court case to consider. At this point, it is necessary for you to use your English skills to locate a court case related to science. Good luck! For help, revisit the You Be the Judge activities in Units 1–5.

1. Describe your court case.

   _____

   _____

   _____

   _____

2. Write three questions for your classmates to answer.

   _____

   _____

   _____

3. Describe any outcomes or decisions that have already been made to present to the class after the discussion.

   _____

   _____

   _____

   _____

# Part 3: Sunspots

## Pre-Listening Activities

With the sun not estimated to burn out for billions of years, most people only think about the sun in terms of how hot it will be on Earth on any given day. There is one phenomenon, however, that occurs on the sun that could impact life on Earth on a daily basis. Sunspots are temporary spots of magnetic fields, sometimes so large they are noticeable with the naked eye as dark areas (although one should never look 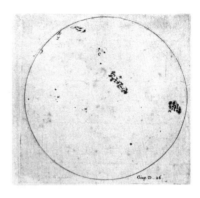 directly at the sun!). These spots are actually cooler than the other parts of the sun, but they can wreak havoc with technology on Earth.

Answer these questions with a partner.

1. Other than heat, what does the sun provide to the planet? Can you guess what the sun is primarily comprised of? Do you know any other characteristics of the sun? Make some guesses or predictions about its composition and size.

   _____

   _____

   _____

2. Sunspots seem to follow an 11-year-long cycle. What can you predict happens at the two extremes—that of much activity and that of lesser activity?

   _____

   _____

   _____

3. If sunspots affect technology, such as satellites, radio waves, and power grids on Earth, what potential ramifications can you predict for the planet?

   _____

   _____

   _____

## Strategy: Listening for and Giving Definitions

There are several strategies instructors will use when defining vocabulary. Being able to identify these strategies will improve your listening comprehension.

Outward (saying the word and then its definition)

> A sunspot is a concentrated magnetic field on the sun that can be identified by its dark color.

Reverse (saying the definition and then the word)

> A concentrated magnetic field on the sun that can be identified by its dark color is a sunspot.

Frequency (saying a frequently used word or phrase first and then a less frequently used word or phrase or vice versa)

> Sunspots can undo—or disrupt—the radio transmissions on Earth.
>
> Sunspots can disrupt—or undo—the radio transmissions on Earth.

Describing (listing details, characteristics, steps, or parts of the word)

> Solar wind consists of both energetic particles and magnetic fields. Both parts come from the sun. They travel at amazingly fast speeds.

Paraphrasing (describing the word in other words)

> According to NASA, solar wind travels in many directions and at supersonic speeds . . . supersonic. In other words, faster than the speed of sound. What is the speed of sound? About 1,100 feet per second.

# Reading

Read the article about the sun. Underline vocabulary words that are new to you.

## Sun

The Sun is a huge, glowing ball at the center of our solar system. The sun provides light, heat, and other energy to Earth. The sun is made up entirely of gas. Most of it is a type of gas that is sensitive to magnetism. This sensitivity makes this type of gas so special that scientists sometimes give it a special name: plasma. Nine planets and their moons, tens of thousands of asteroids, and trillions of comets revolve around the sun. The sun and all these objects are in our solar system. Earth travels around the sun at an average distance of about 92,960,000 miles (149,600,000 kilometers) from it.

The sun's radius (distance from its center to its surface) is about 432,000 miles (695,500 kilometers), approximately 109 times Earth's radius. The following example may help you picture the relative sizes of the sun and Earth and the distance between them: Suppose the radius of Earth were the width of an ordinary paper clip. The radius of the sun would be roughly the height of a desk, and the sun would be about 100 paces from Earth.

The part of the sun that we see has a temperature of about 5500 degrees C (10,000 degrees F). Astronomers measure star temperatures in a metric unit called the Kelvin (abbreviated K). One Kelvin equals exactly 1 Celsius degree (1.8 Fahrenheit degree), but the Kelvin and Celsius scales begin at different points. The Kelvin scale starts at absolute zero, which is -273.15 degrees C (- 459.67 degrees F). Thus, the temperature of the solar surface is about 5800 K. Temperatures in the sun's core reach over 15 million K.

The energy of the sun comes from nuclear fusion reactions that occur deep inside the sun's core. In a fusion reaction, two atomic nuclei join together, creating a new nucleus. Fusion produces energy by converting nuclear matter into energy.

The sun, like Earth, is magnetic. Scientists describe the magnetism of an object in terms of a magnetic field. This is a region that includes all the space occupied by the object and much of the surrounding space. Physicists define a magnetic field as the region in which a magnetic force could be detected—as with a compass. Physicists describe how magnetic an object is in terms of field strength. This is a measure of the force that the field would exert on a magnetic object, such as a compass needle. The typical strength of the sun's field is only about twice that of Earth's field.

But the sun's magnetic field becomes highly concentrated in small regions, with strengths up to 3,000 times as great as the typical strength. These regions shape solar matter to create a variety of features on the sun's surface and in its atmosphere, the part that we can see. These features range from relatively cool, dark structures known as sunspots to spectacular eruptions called flares and coronal mass ejections.

Flares are the most violent eruptions in the solar system. Coronal mass ejections, though less violent than flares, involve a tremendous mass (amount of matter). A single ejection can spew approximately 20 billion tons (18 billion metric tons) of matter into space.

The sun was born about 4.6 billion years ago. It has enough nuclear fuel to remain much as it is for another 5 billion years. Then it will grow to become a type of star called a red giant. Later in the sun's life, it will cast off its outer layers. The remaining core will collapse to become an object called a white dwarf, and will slowly fade. The sun will enter its final phase as a faint, cool object sometimes called a black dwarf.

## Characteristics of the Sun

### Mass and Density

The sun has 99.8 percent of the mass in the solar system. The sun is 333,000 times as massive as Earth. The sun's average density is about 90 pounds per cubic foot (1.4 grams per cubic centimeter). This is about 1.4 times the density of water and less than one-third of Earth's average density.

### Composition

The sun, like most other stars, is made up mostly of atoms of the chemical element hydrogen. The second most plentiful element in the sun is helium, and almost all the remaining matter consists of atoms of seven other elements. For every 1 million atoms of hydrogen in the entire sun, there are 98,000 atoms of helium, 850 of oxygen, 360 of carbon, 120 of neon, 110 of nitrogen, 40 of magnesium, 35 of iron, and 35 of silicon. So about 94 percent of the atoms are hydrogen, and 0.1 percent are elements other than hydrogen and helium.

But hydrogen is the lightest of all elements, and so it accounts for only about 72 percent of the mass. Helium makes up around 26 percent.

The inside of the sun and most of its atmosphere consist of plasma. Plasma is basically a gas whose temperature has been raised to such a high level that it becomes sensitive to magnetism. Scientists sometimes emphasize the difference in behavior between plasma and other gas. They say that plasma is a fourth state of matter, alongside solid, liquid, and gas. But in general, scientists make the distinction between plasma and gas only when technically necessary.

The essential difference between plasma and other gas is an effect of the temperature increase: This increase has made the gas atoms come apart. What is left— the plasma—consists of electrically charged atoms called ions and electrically charged particles called electrons that move about independently.

An electrically neutral atom contains one or more electrons that act as though they form a shell or shells around its central region, its nucleus. Each electron carries a single unit of negative electric charge. Deep inside the atom is the nucleus, which has almost all the atom's mass. The simplest nucleus, that of the most common form of hydrogen, consists of a single particle known as a proton. A proton carries a single unit of positive electric charge. All other nuclei have one or more protons and one or more neutrons. A neutron carries no net charge, and so every nucleus is electrically positive. But a neutral atom has as many electrons as protons. The net electric charge of a neutral atom is therefore zero.

An atom or molecule that comes apart by losing one or more electrons has a positive charge and is called an ion or, sometimes, a positive ion. Most of the atoms inside the sun are positive ions of the most common form of hydrogen. Thus, most of the sun consists of single protons and independent electrons.

The relative amounts of plasma and other gas in a given part of the solar atmosphere depends on the temperature. As the temperature increases, more and more atoms become ionized, and the atoms that are ionized lose more and more electrons. The highest part of the solar atmosphere, called the corona, is strongly ionized. The corona's temperature is usually about 3 million to 5 million K, more than enough to strip away over half the 26 electrons in its iron atoms.

How much of a gas is made up of single atoms and how much of molecules also depends upon its temperature. If the gas is relatively hot, the atoms will move about independently. But if the gas is relatively cool, its atoms may bond (combine chemically), creating molecules. Much of the sun's surface consists of a gas of single atoms. But sunspots are so cool that some of their atoms can bond to form molecules.

Adapted from National Aeronautics and Space Administration, www.nasa.gov/worldbook/sun_worldbook.html. Accessed on February 1, 2010.

## Identifying the Strategy

What strategy is used to introduce the new word in each of these sentences from the reading?

1. The Sun is a huge, glowing ball at the center of our solar system. _____

2. The sun provides light, heat, and other energy to Earth. _____

3. The Kelvin scale starts at absolute zero, which is –273.15 degrees C (–459.67 degrees F). _____

4. The energy of the sun comes from nuclear fusion reactions that occur deep inside the sun's core. In a fusion reaction, two atomic nuclei join together, creating a new nucleus. _____

5. The sun, like Earth, is magnetic. Scientists describe the magnetism of an object in terms of a magnetic field. This is a region that includes all the space occupied by the object and much of the surrounding space. Physicists define a magnetic field as the region in which a magnetic force could be detected—as with a compass. _____

6. These regions shape solar matter to create a variety of features on the sun's surface and in its atmosphere, the part that we can see. _____

7. These features range from relatively cool, dark structures known as sunspots to spectacular eruptions called flares and coronal mass ejections. _____

8. Then it will grow to become a type of star called a red giant. _____

9. What is left—the plasma—consists of electrically charged atoms called ions and electrically charged particles called electrons that move about independently. _____

## Giving Definitions

Reread the second part of the reading that begins on page 214. If you were delivering this as a presentation, what would you choose to rewrite so that definitions would be easier to understand? Choose five sentences and rewrite them using one of the strategies from the box on page 212.

1. _____

_____

_____

2. _____

_____

_____

3. _____

_____

_____

4. _____

_____

_____

5. _____

_____

_____

Compare your answers with a small group. What terms did you choose to define or better define? Why did you choose the same (or different) sentences?

## Note-Taking

### Strategy: Taking Notes on New Words

It's easy to panic when you hear a word you are not familiar with in a lecture. You may worry that you don't know how to spell it and then you may miss the definition. Or you may draw a blank and not know what to write down. You may also see it on a visual and concentrate on copying it, but then miss the definition when it is described or paraphrased. Some strategies for dealing with new vocabulary are suggested.

✓ Write only the first letter or first few letters you know. Then write the definition that the instructor uses. You can look up the spelling later.

✓ Put a star or some other notation by the new word so you can check the spelling or definition later.

✓ Write the word phonetically—the way it sounds. That can help figure out the spelling later.

✓ Concentrate on the root of the word and not the prefixes or suffixes. From the definition, you can determine the affixes later.

✓ Write new terms in the margin so they will be easy to go back and find later.

### Taking Notes with New Words

Think of three technical words from your own field of study, and write their definitions. Read them to a partner so he or she can practice writing them. Then reverse roles and practice writing the new vocabulary your partner is teaching you. What strategies worked best for you?

Your Words and Definitions

_____

_____

_____

Your Partner's Words and Definitions

_____

_____

_____

## 🏋 Vocabulary Power

There are a number of terms and phrases in this lecture that you may encounter in other academic settings. Add at least five vocabulary items to your vocabulary notebook or log.

Match the words in bold from the lecture on the left with a definition on the right.

1. ____ Today I'd like to talk about a unique **phenomenon** that takes place on the sun.

2. ____ At this time, the sun is almost continually dotted with spots, and **it is plagued by** flare eruptions.

3. ____ A coronal mass ejection is a mammoth cloud of hot plasma **hurled** into space from the sun.

4. ____ What isn't known is the **havoc** that can be wreaked on Earth . . .

5. ____ Some recordkeeping indicates that there was actually a **relatively** long period of inactivity that counters the normal 11-year cycle.

6. ____ Three days **prior**, astronomers witnessed an explosion on the sun.

7. ____ But as the solar storm **subsided**, so did its results on Earth.

8. ____ With the way technology is growing, are we prepared for a solar storm of such **magnitude** again?

a. suffers from

b. chaos or destruction

c. earlier

d. an event that can be watched

e. lessened

f. size

g. to some extent

h. thrown

## Listening 3: Sunspots

**Listening to a Lecture**

The listening passage is a lecture from an astronomy class. The instructor is discussing sunspots and their possible ramifications to life on Earth. Throughout the lecture, he introduces new terms and their definitions.  Use the space to write notes. Concentrate on new vocabulary and try some of the new strategies.

surface          Santp    Canada          florida

11  ~~better~~ part          power closed
                             many areas.
  facts                         (99)
  ~~electricity~~
  of beginning                 1998 = banking machen
  continual
                               1/0s
  5 gas                        the really cost
                               we prepared
    Hot gas.                   2008   recycle
  energy far/Mars                      >/or22
    far far away
  other space.
  faster than normal
    technology.
      one works
    ↑ Ne good reason
    global perspective.
      critical
      16:55
      17:15                  1989.   huge crowd of gas
        11 cycle

**Checking Your Understanding: Main Ideas**

Review your notes. Listen again to the lecture if necessary, and then put a check mark (✓) next to the statements that best reflect the main ideas.

_____ Sunspots occur on the sun, but affect life on Earth more than one might think.

_____ The two extremes of solar activity, minimum and maximum, are when Earth is affected.

_____ Technology is a victim of solar storms, both in space and on Earth.

_____ Sunspot cycles occur every 11 years and remain fairly predictable.

_____ Results of solar cycles have primarily occurred in the modern day.

_____ With the recent onslaught of technological development, Earth may not be ready for another storm.

**Checking Your Understanding: Details**

Using your notes, circle the best answer.

1. What is true about sunspots?

    a. They are cooler, dark magnetic fields.

    b. They are part of the sun's composition.

    c. They make life quiet on Earth.

    d. They aren't visible to the naked eye.

2. What happens with solar flare activity diminishes?

    a. Hot gases increase.

    b. Sunspots decrease.

    c. Coronal ejections take place.

    d. Technology problems rise.

3. What is the best definition of a coronal mass ejection?

   a. a gas thrown from the Earth

   b. a cloud of gas around the sun

   c. a huge gas cloud thrown from Earth

   d. a huge gas cloud thrown from the sun

4. What is the best synonym for *bombard*?

   a. assault

   b. destruction

   c. brush

   d. search

5. What happens when something deteriorates?

   a. It loses money.

   b. It wears off.

   c. It falls apart.

   d. It ends.

6. What was the catalyst that caused Quebec's power to fail?

   a. electricity

   b. an explosion

   c. energy

   d. a provocation

7. What is plasma?

   a. northern lights

   b. a gas with charged particles

   c. a gas in Earth's magnetic field

   d. currents or movements

## Discussion

In the video, the students brainstormed and expressed which ideas they liked and why. They also admitted a lack of information when they couldn't remember the details. Being able to have strong reasons for what you consider to be a priority and being able to professionally reject others' ideas is an important skill to master in academic discussions.

Imagine you are a team of astronomers who have discovered a new planet in the solar system. You believe there is life on this new planet and the inhabitants of such a planet are very different than Earthlings. Brainstorm a list of attributes that these new people have.

Attributes of the Inhabitants of the New Planet

_____

_____

_____

_____

_____

You've now been told by your boss at NASA that not all of the attributes should be announced in the first press release about the discovery. Work with your team to choose only three attributes to include in the press release. Be prepared to explain why you've selected these three items for inclusion.

Our Top Three

_____

_____

_____

**Rapid Vocabulary Review**

From the three answers on the right, circle the one that best explains, is an example of, or combines with the vocabulary item on the left as it is used in this unit.

| Vocabulary | Answers | | |
|---|---|---|---|
| Synonyms | | | |
| 1. roughly | exactly | correctly | approximately |
| 2. revolve | move around | move through | move down |
| 3. magnitude | price | size | focus |
| 4. appealing | confusing | attractive | industrious |
| 5. the peak | the high point | the main attraction | the small detail |
| 6. fade | put on carefully | become lighter | make heavier |
| 7. strip away | add on | remove | keep after |
| 8. draw a blank | not have any money | ask for a favor | not have any idea |
| 9. prior | before | traditional | important |
| 10. miniature | small | familiar | academic |
| 11. a forecast | a concept | a prediction | a response |
| 12. deteriorate | have more money | create problems | become worse |
| Combinations and Associations | | | |
| 13. bring a company to its ___ | knees | feet | legs |
| 14. ___ precedence (over) | make | put | take |
| 15. first ___, first served | arrive | come | seated |
| 16. the sun ___ | subsides | sets | struggles |
| 17. the naked ___ | face | arm | eye |
| 18. ___ priority to | make | give | take |
| 19. a ___ topic | warm | medium | hot |
| 20. ___ a distinction between X and Y | make | leave | put |

# ⇨✕⊐ Synthesizing: Projects and Presentations

| Short In-Class Speaking Assignments | Longer Outside Assignments |
|---|---|
| I'm an amateur . . . | The Planets and Stars |
| Prepare a short two-minute presentation on a hobby or activity at which you are an amateur. Include details about why you don't do this professionally. | Work with a small group and choose one of the planets or a star to research. Prepare a presentation on the planet you have chosen. Include details about the planet's composition, statistics, and other interesting phenomenon. State why the details you chose were priorities for you. Consider using visual aids to make your presentation more interesting. Be prepared to take questions from the audience and answer as best you can (admit a lack of information when you make a guess). |
| If I Were an Astronaut | Survey |
| Make an impromptu speech about what you would do if you were an astronaut. Where would you go? Why? | Work with a group to create a survey about where or what space missions should next explore. Give your survey to 10 people and then bring your results to class. Combine your data and generate visual aids based on your results. Then prepare a presentation drawing conclusions about why people made the choices they did. Present your visual aids to the class. Include some demographic information such as age and gender. |

## Vocabulary Log

To increase your vocabulary knowledge, write a definition or translation for each vocabulary item. Then write an original phrase, sentence, or note that will help you remember the vocabulary item.

| Vocabulary Item | Definition or Translation | Your Original Phrase, Sentence, or Note |
|---|---|---|
| 1. a compass | an instrument for direction | A compass points to the directions N, S, E, and W. |
| 2. subside | | |
| 3. disrupt | | |
| 4. to hurl | | |
| 5. promptly | | |
| 6. composition | | |
| 7. density | | |
| 8. a phenomenon | | |
| 9. to brief | | |
| 10. mammoth (adj) | | |
| 11. signify | | |
| 12. beyond | | |
| 13. bid (n.) | | |
| 14. glow | | |

| Vocabulary Item | Definition or Translation | Your Original Phrase, Sentence, or Note |
|---|---|---|
| 15. stem from | | |
| 16. phenomenon | | |
| 17. the onslaught of | | |
| 18. brief (v.) | | |
| 19. spot (n.) | | |
| 20. amateur | | |
| 21. to plague | | |
| 22. hot topic | | |
| 23. wreak havoc with | | |
| 24. an eclipse | | |
| 25. to track | | |